Out of the Ashes

Out of the Ashes

The restoration of a burned boy

Peter Gladwin
with Jan Greenough

MONARCH
BOOKS

Oxford, UK & Grand Rapids, Michigan, USA

Published by Monarch Books
an imprint of
Lion Hudson plc
Wilkinson House, Jordan Hill Road,
Oxford OX2 8DR, England
Email: monarch@lionhudson.com
www.lionhudson.com/monarch

ISBN 978 1 85424 992 0 (print)
ISBN 978 0 85721 240 5 (epub)
ISBN 978 0 85721 239 9 (Kindle)

First edition 2011

Acknowledgments
Unless otherwise stated, Scripture quotations taken from the *Holy Bible,
New International Version*, copyright © 1973, 1978, 1984 by the International
Bible Society. Used by permission of Zondervan and Hodder & Stoughton
Limited. All rights reserved. The 'NIV' and 'New International Version'
trademarks are registered in the United States Patent and Trademark
Office by International Bible Society. Use of either trademark requires the
permission of International Bible Society. UK trademark number 1448790.

A catalogue record for this book is available from the British Library.

Printed and bound in the UK, May 2017, LH26

Contents

I would like to dedicate this book to my Mum and Dad, who experienced a harsh upbringing themselves and didn't know any other way of life.

Foreword

If I was a betting man, I would have said that from the word "go" the odds were pretty much stacked against Peter's life. From being horrifically burned and scarred in a house fire as a baby, to being surrounded in his childhood by serious violence, petty crime, and a heavy drinking and drug taking culture, he was destined to be either seriously depressed, dead, or in and out of prison for most of his adult life.

Peter's story is, however, one of the most compelling biographies I have ever read, and it doesn't end where you would expect it to! Far from being yet another crime statistic or ending up on a slab in a morgue after a fight (and that could easily have happened), Peter tells us his story of triumph over adversity. This story gives us a profound demonstration that having the odds stacked against you at one point in your life doesn't have to dictate your future. In a remarkable and frankly miraculous turnaround, despite incredible and devastating adversity, Peter is now a living demonstration of hope.

Just what happened to cause such a radical transformation is for you to read on and find out. I will just say that as for me, I finished reading this book feeling encouraged, full of hope, and in awe. If you know anyone who needs "hope", anyone who has the odds stacked against them, then I suggest that you send them a copy of this book. However, I also suggest that you take time to read it yourself. You'll probably find it hard to put down. Be mindful though, this isn't just a good read, the contents of this book may just change your life.

Carl Beech
General Director
CVM

Acknowledgments

First I would like to thank Lynne Pugh, the artist and teacher who guided my first attempts to tell my own story, and who worked so hard to help me, despite her own illness.

Next, Bill Partington from UCB, who came into Café Oasis and heard my story: he took it to Tony Collins at Monarch Books.

Jan Greenough, my co-author, who made me relive some of the most painful and the most joyful episodes in my life to tell the story you read here.

My sister Annette, who shared a message with me that even today is transforming my life.

And finally and most importantly my amazing wife Sarah, for her patient and loyal support and encouragement, for our three wonderful children and for helping to build a solid foundation for our family life.

Chapter 1

Out of the ashes

"You be a good girl and look after the boys," said Mum. "I'll only be next door if you want me."

Mum liked to go next door for a cup of tea some afternoons – she said it was the only break she got. "Three kids in the house and another one on the way," she said to her friend Sheila. "It's a good job I've got Annette."

"She's a proper little mother," agreed Sheila, "even at four. How are you feeling?"

"Tired," said Mum. "Seven months gone now. Too big to be chasing after toddlers."

In fact my brother John was the only toddler – he was two, and he started whining as soon as Mum went out. But Mum knew Annette would soon calm him down. She'd left them both eating bread and jam at the table. I was the baby, just under a year old, and at least I wasn't walking yet. She knew I'd stay where she put me, lying on the hearth rug. She'd lit the fire and got it drawing up nicely with some sheets of newspaper, so I'd be warm enough.

She settled herself down in Sheila's armchair. "I left the Yale on the latch. They'll be all right for half an hour."

She wasn't a bad mother. But the babies had come along so fast, and she was always worried about money, and what her husband was up to – usually at the bookie's or the pub, drinking his benefit money. Sometimes she was desperate for a minute's peace.

"This is lovely," she said, stirring her tea. "Just what I needed."

A minute later she heard screaming. Annette was banging frantically on the front door.

"Oh, what now?" she said. Sheila opened the door and Annette ran in, dragging John crying behind her. For a minute or two they couldn't make any sense of what she was saying, between her sobs.

"Fire, Mummy! The rug's on fire! I couldn't get hold of Peter – too much flames…"

Mum had been holding John and trying to quieten him down. Now she thrust him into Sheila's arms and ran outside. "The baby!"

She pushed at her own front door but it didn't move.

"I left it on the latch!" she shouted. "How can it be locked?" She kicked and hammered on the door, but she realized what must have happened. When Annette ran out, the door had slammed behind her, knocking the Yale catch out of position. The keys were inside where she had left them. The front window seemed to be full of smoke.

"Call the fire brigade!" she yelled at Sheila. Then she looked round desperately. She had to get in the house somehow. Under the window there was a heavy wooden hatch to the coal cellar. She lifted it and clambered awkwardly over the wooden rim, but it was no good. Her pregnant belly was too huge to fit in the small opening. Tears were streaming down Mum's face. "Peter! My baby!" she kept sobbing.

She heard sirens and the fire engine arrived. The firemen ran to fix up hoses. One of them led her away, crying and shaking, back to Sheila's house, but she wouldn't go inside. It seemed a long time before they broke the door down, and by then flames and smoke were coming out of the upstairs windows. They trained the hoses in through the hall: everything in the house would be wet.

When the flames finally died down she wanted to run over and see, but Sheila held her back. She saw one fireman shaking his head as another one went in to search the house. There was a horrible smell of wet ash and soot. The street was filling up as people came out of their houses to see what was going on, and an ambulance came screeching up the street. Two neighbours stood by Sheila's doorstep, talking.

"The baby was in there, you know."

"Poor little soul. Terrible way to die. Mary'll never get over it."

The street went quiet as the fireman came out again; his big body and padded jacket seemed to fill up the doorway. His leather gauntlets looked huge and clumsy, but he was holding a tiny blackened body with great gentleness. He looked up and shouted, "Get some medical help over here! He's alive!"

Chapter 2

Lost boy

My earliest memory: I'm lying on my back, surrounded by chaos – people, noise, banging and loud voices – and lights are flashing past overhead. Surely I can't be remembering that first traumatic journey, being rushed on a trolley along hospital corridors? More likely it's a memory I've put together from many experiences, because I was in and out of hospital for about four years. Most of those trips were planned ones, because I had to have a long series of reconstructive operations. But some of them may have been emergencies, when I fell and split the delicate new skin grafts over and over again.

I was in hospital for a long time to start with. When I was admitted no one expected me to live: my skin and clothes had blackened and fused together. I was charred from head to toe, but the worst damage was on my left side, which had been nearest to the fire. It took some time before my condition was stable enough for me to survive the operating theatre, where the surgeons began to try to salvage what they could of my burned limbs. I had amputations on both feet – all my toes and part of each foot for about a quarter of its length. All the fingers on my left hand were taken off. I had 75 per cent burns on my legs and body, so I've got huge scars everywhere, including my face and what remains of my left ear. It's thanks to the amazing skill of the doctors and nurses of St Luke's

14

Hospital in Bradford that I'm here at all.

I suppose my mother must have visited me, but she had two other children at home and another on the way, so travelling to and fro wouldn't have been easy. For any baby, separation from its mother is traumatic, but I guess that probably paled into insignificance beside the intense pain I was always suffering. Once I was discharged, I was taken home in a pushchair, which was where I spent most of the next four years. I couldn't learn to walk like other children, because I had no feet, and I was always bandaged to protect my healing skin.

We lived in King Cross, Halifax, in a terraced council house with three bedrooms – Mum and Dad and whichever baby was newest shared one room, and the rest of us shared the others. We were a big family: there were three children when the fire happened in 1960 (Annette, John and me), and Susan was born a couple of months later. Tony was born in 1961, when I was two, June in 1962, David in 1963 and James in 1964. Then there was a gap of seven years before our last brother, Adrian, was born in 1971. Mum struggled to cope, but she was always pregnant or nursing a new baby, and she couldn't keep an eye on everything at once. With all those children in the house and the rough and tumble of family life, even when I was sitting in my pushchair it was easy for me to get bumped – and every knock meant that the skin would split and bleed, and I'd be back to the Burns Clinic for new dressings.

The operations were the worst part of it: I screamed whenever they took me back into the hospital, because I knew I would wake up in even more pain. The one thing I wanted when I was little was for the pain to go away; as soon as I was old enough to have some idea of the future, I was looking forward to the time when I wouldn't be hurting. Someone must have told me that one day I would get better. But it was a long time coming.

By the time Mum was pregnant with James, when I was four, she couldn't cope any more: seven active children plus one with a disability was too much. She sent me to live with my Grandma and Grandad.

It was bliss. Even at four years old, I was able to appreciate the difference between their home and ours. For a start, it was quiet: at home there was always a baby screaming. For another thing, I had my Grandma's undivided attention. Mum was always too busy to bring me things or play with me, so I relied on Annette if I wanted a drink or something to eat. Grandma talked to me, played with me, and read to me. Their house wasn't grand. Just like home, it was a terrace-house with steps down to a tiny yard with an outside toilet.

Grandad was a man of few words, but I wasn't afraid of him. He never said it, but somehow I always knew he loved me. He worked in the coal yard, and he used to come home at night as black as if he'd been down the pit, wearing a leather jacket which protected his clothes from the heavy coal sacks he hauled around on his shoulder all day. He had a special chair – the only armchair in the house – and no one else ever sat there. Grandma always sat on a hard chair by the table.

When I was four, the operations came to an end, and about a year later I started learning to walk. I was so proud to be getting upright at last. What I wanted more than anything else was to be able to run around like my brothers and sisters, and join in their games. First I had to be fitted with a pair of special boots, adapted to stay on my feet with a metal brace that went round my ankle. They were cruelly uncomfortable, and the metal bit into my skin, but I would put up with anything if it meant I could start walking. In the physiotherapy room at the hospital there were two parallel metal bars, and a nurse would prop me up between them so I could support most of my weight on my arms. The metal was cold and hurt the tender skin of my hands, and of course I couldn't grip properly with my fingerless left hand. But gradually I started taking more and more of my weight on my feet, and shifting one foot at a time in the heavy boots. The nurse knelt at the other end of the bars to catch me and turn me round. I can remember her voice, cajoling and encouraging me: "That's right, Peter! Come towards me. Good boy! One more step, now. You can do it."

I went on having monthly appointments at the Outpatients Department of the Burns Unit until I was ten, and I used to dread them. I was constantly being refitted for new boots, and I hated the doctors touching my feet. Something about the healing process meant that the skin was extremely sensitive, and it was terribly painful when they peeled off the protective gauze which covered the misshapen stumps where my feet should have been. Still, much as I hated them, those boots did the trick, and I learned to walk fairly normally. People are often amazed when they find out the extent of the damage to my feet, and wonder how I manage to balance without toes.

I'm always amused when I hear athletes talking about "going through the pain barrier". I'll never be an athlete, but I knew all about that when I was five. I was determined to learn to walk, and I had to strengthen the wasted muscles in my legs by practising as much as I could. I practised in the hospital and I practised at home, feeling my way round the furniture in Grandma's house like a toddler, and taking a few steps unsupported between a table and a chair.

Sometimes Mum and Dad used to come and visit. The adults would all sit round the table smoking and drinking tea, while I played on the floor by their feet. It was safe to do that there, because there weren't any other children to trip over me. But as I healed and grew stronger, the babies at home were growing up, too. Mum and Dad had finally got to the top of the housing list, and their big family had qualified them for a new house with more bedrooms. On one of their visits they told Grandma and Grandad they thought they could manage to have me back.

I loved my grandparents, and I'll always be grateful to them for taking me in, but I wanted to go home, too. I didn't have any friends because I'd always been confined to the house or my pushchair, and I longed to be able to play out in the street with the other kids. I went home for a weekend at first (which was probably a trial run for my Mum as much as for me), and when that went all right, I went for a week or so, and eventually I moved back home.

The new house was great. It was in Illingworth, several miles away, but still part of Halifax. The houses on this estate were semi-detached, and ours was on the corner of the road, so our garden wrapped right round the side of the house. It was a fantastic place for a small boy to explore – especially if you'd been confined to the house for most of your life. I loved being able to walk on the grass right down to the farthest corner of the garden, under a towering privet hedge. It didn't matter to me that the grass was never cut, and the privet was never trimmed, so the whole place looked like a wilderness. It was paradise.

The other exciting thing was starting primary school. I missed out the infants' school completely, and started at Moorside Junior School when I was seven. I knew I was way behind the other kids – they'd all been at school for two or three years already, and they could read – but once again I was determined to make the best of things. I'd already faced a lot of challenges in my young life, and I was always prepared to work hard to keep up with other people. Fortunately Grandma had read to me a lot (there wasn't much else I could do when I couldn't move about) and I think that must have helped. The words seemed to make sense to me, and I soon caught up with the class in reading.

When I saw the other boys playing football in the playground I longed to be one of them – but who would choose the kid with the funny boots to be on their team? I learned to run and even to kick a ball (that was excruciating at first), and when we had PE I managed to get by without drawing too much attention to myself. In fact, one day our class was due to play football against another class, and amazingly, I was on the team. I was so excited. Dad had managed to get hold of a pair of old boots and stuffed the toes with newspaper. They were agony to wear, but I didn't care. In the end I never played – the match was cancelled due to bad weather, or something – and I was terribly disappointed. But deep inside I knew I could have done it, if only I'd had the chance.

All I ever wanted was to fit in, to be the same as the other kids. Of course, there was never much chance of that. My scarred face and misshapen ear marked me out, and so did my heavy boots with their steel toecaps and metal braces. But the worst thing of all was swimming. At least in the classroom the boots hid my feet, and my clothes covered the mass of scar tissue and skin grafts on my body and legs. At the swimming pool I couldn't hide any of it.

I'd never been swimming before, but there was a pool in the school grounds, and everyone was expected to learn to swim. In the first lesson I cowered at the back of the line of kids by the edge of the pool, acutely aware of the stares and sniggers and whispers of my classmates. The teacher called me out to the front and told me to jump into the water. When I hesitated, terrified, he hit me with a slipper, so that I overbalanced and fell in. Everyone laughed. All I could do was pretend I didn't care.

I made out that I didn't care about the names they called me, too: "Spaz", "Crip", "Fingers" and "Spud feet". I knew there was nothing I could do about it.

School was hard work, and I felt very isolated by my difference, but I did have one or two friends to hang out with. Mike Davis[1] was my best friend – I called him Davey – and he didn't make fun of me as much as the others. He was a scruffy kid, too, and I think that his clothes, like mine, came from the YMCA second-hand clothes pile. We recognized each other – we were two of a kind. Davey's house was even more of a wreck than ours was.

1   Note: The names of some individuals have been changed to preserve anonymity.

My Dad never had a job in his life – all he'd ever known was living on benefits. As soon as he got his money every week he'd be off to the betting shop and the pub, and once the pubs closed he'd come home with a few mates and get the card tables out. The men would sit round in a haze of cigarette smoke, and throw wads of money onto the table. I don't know how much cash changed hands on those nights, but I know my Dad never seemed to win. Mum used to go through his pockets afterwards and take what was left to pay the tallyman – the few bits of furniture we had were all bought on "tick".

My Mum was the family breadwinner. She usually worked as a packer in a factory, though from time to time she would disappear out of our lives. Sometimes she went off with a boyfriend, sometimes she just walked out because she'd had another row with Dad. Generally, when we came home from school in the afternoon, Mum would be out at work. If Dad had been lucky with the horses he'd be in the pub drinking his winnings; if he'd lost he'd be at home in a bad mood, so we tried to keep out of his way. He always had a few beers while he was betting, so he was quite likely to be sleeping it off on the sofa. Annette had the door key on a string round her neck, and she would let us all in and we'd creep round trying not to disturb him.

We were always hungry. We lived off the bare basics – tomatoes on toast or beans on toast. Dad loved his fish and chips, so sometimes one of us would be sent down to the chippy. There was never anything much in the pantry – a bit of cheese, margarine and jam. Tea was bread and scrape – the dripping left over from a roast. At the weekend we sometimes had chicken (especially when Mum was working in the chicken packing factory) but Mum wasn't much of a cook. I especially hated her porridge, because she always burned it, but I had to eat it: if I complained, I'd get a slap.

She wasn't much of a housewife, either – I suppose with nine kids to feed, the state of the house was the least of her worries. The house was always cold, because we had no money for coal. We all shared beds, and they didn't get changed very often. We didn't have carpets, only bare boards, and no one bothered to sweep up. I remember once bringing a friend home from school and suddenly noticing that there was a bit of stale bread on the floor – goodness knows how long it had been there – and I felt embarrassed. I knew homes weren't supposed to be like ours. But I didn't know how you made it any different.

When I was seven we moved to another new house, and for a while it was lovely: the clean new paintwork made it look light and airy, and it was warm because it had central heating. But we boys were always up to mischief. Once when we were messing about in the attic we stepped off a roof-joist and crashed through into our bedroom below. I remember landing on the bed in a cloud of dust, with chunks of plaster all over the floor, and looking up at the gaping hole in the ceiling with the bare light-bulb dangling beside it. As usual, when Dad got home he wasn't in a fit state to notice anything, but we all got a beating next day when he sobered up and saw the mess.

It wasn't long before we'd trashed the whole house. The toilets were filthy, the kitchen was a tip, the paintwork was all chipped and bashed about and the little kids had drawn on the walls. We were one of those families that the council despairs of – they moved us on when we outgrew a house, or the neighbours complained about the noise and the kids' behaviour. They would put us in a new house but it wouldn't be long before the same thing would happen all over again, and they'd have another property to clean up and repair.

It was a violent household, too. My Mum had a very short fuse, especially where I was concerned. I seemed to get on her nerves, and she hit me so often that even if she raised her hand to push her hair back I would flinch. I suppose she was short-tempered because she was always tired. No one ever talked about my disability, or mentioned how I got injured so badly – it was one of those things that you just didn't do. But one night I overheard my parents arguing. They were both drunk, and blaming each other. "It's your fault he's the way he is," my Dad said. "You went out and left him by that fire." Then my Mum started going on about the fact that he hadn't been there either. I think they both felt guilty, and it made them angry.

Violence was part of our lives. We lived on some pretty rough estates, so we were used to seeing drunken fights outside pubs, and people shouting abuse at their neighbours. One day I was going past the playing field near our house when I saw Dad fighting another man. A crowd had gathered to watch, and the men were clawing at each other's eyes with their fingers, until another man picked up a log and hit my Dad round the back of his head. A gang of little kids were shouting "Kill him!" Another day I was in the school playground and saw Dad come in and pick a fight with the PE teacher because of something he'd said to one of my brothers.

When you grow up in that sort of atmosphere, you don't know any different: you think it's just normal, the way life is. There was no one to be a role model (at least, not in a positive way); there were no values. It was just survival of the fittest – you did whatever you wanted, when you wanted to, and you fought to get the biggest bit of blanket or the best bit of food, and you elbowed your brother out of the way to get it. No one set boundaries or taught you to share, or wait, or think about anyone else.

Mum and Dad had probably been brought up the same way. Somehow they stayed married, but it was a troubled, uneasy affair, full of rows and fights. They both had relationships with other people. I suppose they had the same attitude as the rest of us: take what you want, because otherwise you'll have nothing. And like everyone, they were looking for reassurance that they were worth something, that someone valued them. It's easy to get drawn into casual sex when you're desperate for warmth, companionship and affirmation.

I had my first sexual relationship when I was only ten years old: a sixteen-year-old girl took me to a derelict house and told me what she wanted to do. I went along with it, confused and flattered that she wanted to be with me. The difference in our ages suggests to me now that the relationship was entirely exploitative – she went with my eleven-year-old brother John, too – and she must have had her own problems, to be seeking to experiment with children so much younger. But it says something about our lives in those days: the lack of parental supervision, the exposure to casual sex, the neediness and the longing for love, affirmation and security. I often wonder how

I emerged without serious psychological damage, and can only conclude that God's hand was on my life.

Naturally, we copied the behaviour of the adults around us. Dad did occasional spells in prison, always for shoplifting. He wasn't a serious criminal, just a habitual thief, always looking for a quick way to get something for nothing. Our first television was a pay-to-view rented one, with a money box like a gas meter: you had to put a shilling in the slot before it would switch on. Dad broke into it so we could watch for free. He'd take the coins out of the back and feed them into the front again. It was the same principle with gas and electricity meters. We watched and learned, and soon John and I could get into a gas meter in no time.

John was a huge influence on me. Although he was only a year older he always seemed to be craftier and more streetwise, and he was always showing me how to do things. In spite of my humiliation in school swimming lessons, I loved to swim – but we never had any money to go to the public baths. John found out how to break into the school pool, and we often went and had our own private swim there.

Because we knew the school building, it was the obvious place for our first burglary together. We broke in the day before the Harvest Festival, when the hall was full of produce, laid out in baskets and boxes on the stage. For a couple of kids who were always hungry, it was heaven. We ate loads of apples, oranges and bananas (we never saw fruit at home) and took bags full of tins and biscuits home with us, so everyone could have some. It was great: I felt as if I'd done something really clever, getting all this nice stuff for the family to eat.

I didn't feel so good the next day. When we all went into assembly the head teacher told us he had a serious announcement to make:

"Last night someone broke into our school hall and took many of the harvest gifts you have been bringing in." There were gasps of horror from the other kids. "I'm sorry to tell you that our Harvest Festival is ruined. Usually we make up boxes of food to give to the old people who live locally, people who are needy and sometimes don't get enough to eat. They are always so pleased when you go out in groups to visit them and take them your gifts. This year that won't be happening, and they will go without."

For the first time, I knew what it was to feel guilty.

Later that day, John and I were called into the Head's office, where a policeman was waiting for us. He asked John to take off his shoe, and he showed us how it matched a footprint John had left on a table when we climbed in through the window. Because John was eleven, he was old enough to be arrested and charged.

I was shocked to realize that we were in trouble with the police, but when John got off with a caution I cheered up. I learned a valuable lesson that day: it was OK to take stuff, because nothing much happened to you even if you got caught. And of course, if you were clever, you didn't get caught at all.

One day John told me he'd got some buried treasure. We got a spade and went off to a field, and started digging behind some bushes. It was a bit like a game of pirates, but for real: sure enough, the spade clunked onto a metal box, and when we got it out it was the coin box off a gas meter that he'd buried there. John emptied it and shared out the shillings with me.

I'd never had any money before, and it was great to be able to go and buy all the sweets I wanted, or get some chips when I was hungry. I told my mate Davey and soon we were breaking into houses and doing a meter most weeks. We never got caught. We even did a few extra jobs when it was coming up to Christmas, so we'd have more money. I remember we went down to the local toy shop and bought loads of stuff – a couple of bikes and some plastic machine guns. I think the shop owner was a bit suspicious but he didn't say anything. We were running up a serious number of burglaries between us – but we were still young enough to want to spend the money on toys.

The only time I got worried was once when we were in a house we thought was empty. I was in the hall when I heard an old lady call out from upstairs, "Is that you, Eric?" I froze on the spot. For a moment I couldn't move, but then Davey grabbed my arm and we ran out of the back door. I felt cold with fear. What if the old lady had come down and seen us? What if she'd had a heart attack and we were to blame?

When I was eleven, John and I tried to run away from home. I can't remember why, or where we thought we would go, but we knew we'd need some money, so we broke into a bookmaker's shop. I was small and skinny, so I was always the one to climb in through tiny windows, and on this occasion I had to climb up what I thought was a drainpipe, but it turned out to be a fat cable running up the side of the building. It gave me a fright when it snapped, but I managed to get a handhold on the windowsill and climb in. Then I let John in.

Unfortunately, our parents had reported us missing and the police were already looking out for us. John might have got away with it, but I was easy to spot, with all my scars. They knew we'd done a job that day because we had all the money on us. When I got to the police station I found that Davey had been arrested, too. It was quite exciting really – it felt like being in a film, with the police questioning us as if we were big criminals. By that time we'd done so many jobs that we couldn't remember them all, so we agreed with whatever the police suggested. They eventually charged me with 101 offences – I think we helped them out a lot with their clear-up rate that day!

It took a while for the case to come to court because of all the evidence they had to collect, so I was taken to the Crown Court and remanded in custody. No one was going to let such a prolific offender go free, even if he was only eleven. I spent eight weeks in Thorp Arch Remand Centre, locked up most of the day except for an exercise period. I suspect the aim was to frighten me off from ever going anywhere near prison again, but actually I quite liked it. The cell was warm and clean, I got three meals a day (more food than I ever saw at home), and there was a little counter where you could buy sweets and toothpaste and things. I didn't get into trouble (who was going to bother with a little eleven-year-old boy?) so there was actually less violence than there was at home. No one hit me all the time I was there. Most of all, I found a sort of identity: I was with a lot of criminals, and I had a peer group and people to admire and imitate. Not a bad way of life, I thought.

Still, I knew it wasn't supposed to be like that. While I was inside I wrote a poem:

> *There was a boy called Peter*
> *Every day he broke into a gas meter*
> *Every time he did a job,*
> *He always did it on his tod.*
> *One day as he was in a house,*
> *He saw a little horrible mouse*
> *He said: "Go away you horrible creature*
> *You remind me of an awful teacher."*
> *Just as he was about to retire*
> *He tripped over the rug and fell in the fire*
> *Now Peter is dead and gone*
> *But I will always remember his song*
> *I can just hear him say*
> *Always remember crime doesn't pay.*

When my case came up at last there wasn't much the judge could do with me. I got twelve months' supervision, which meant that once a week I had to report to the Probation Office. Sometimes they had a chat with me, but mostly they just ticked the box to say that I'd attended. Once again, as far as I was concerned there were no real consequences to my actions.

Back at home, things went on much the same. We got evicted a couple of times because the family was causing problems, and each time we were moved to rougher and rougher estates, ending up in a street called Furness Avenue, living in an old green prefab. The place had a bad reputation: people who lived there were known locally as the "tin house people".

The fights and squalor were making my home life unbearable, mostly because now I was old enough to have some idea that life didn't have to be like that.

When I was twelve Dad got a three-month prison sentence for theft. The first we knew of it was when we came home from school to find Social Services waiting for us. Mum had gone off with a boyfriend some weeks previously, so the local authority decided that we would all have to go into children's homes. It was brilliant – even better than prison. I had my own room, plenty of food, friends my own age, and really nice carers.

After a couple of months I heard that Mum had reappeared. She was staying with my Uncle Joe in Halifax and getting some of the kids back. I was allowed to go home for a weekend, and although I'd enjoyed being in the children's home, it was great to be back with the family. I loved my Mum and my brothers and sisters, even though we didn't really have ways of showing it. I was disappointed when I had to go back to the children's home – especially as it seemed as if everyone else was staying.

A few days later I told my carers that I was going out on my bike, and pedalled several miles back to Mum's. I had a great day with the family, then Social Services came and picked me up and took me back. I was upset, but I think my Mum had called them. My relationship with her was a strange one: I think she was never sure if she really wanted me around.

After that I was fostered for a while by a really lovely couple. That was when I saw what home life could be like. They had a clean house and a tidy garden (that was a surprise) and no one ever seemed to shout or fight. They were kind to me, and bought me a sort of go-kart so I could ride down the hill outside the house. But once again that time came to an end. Dad was out of prison and had got back together with Mum, and they'd been allocated a huge house in Hebden Bridge. I went home again to watch my family reduce yet another house from smart and new to a broken-down wreck.

Over the next four years I made my way through secondary school without achieving very much. I had started out at Ovenden West Riding School, which I hated – my happiest day was when I walked up the road towards it and saw smoke coming out of the roof, where someone had set it on fire. After our latest move I went to Calder High School in Mytholmroyd. It was a rough school and I was a rough kid, and the teachers never expected any of us to come to anything. I used to get into trouble for kicking off in class, and those were the days when you still got the strap – six blows across the palm of your hand. It was no surprise that I left school with no qualifications. I couldn't wait to get out into the world and get a job. Maybe I'd be able to get away from home, too, one day.

Chapter 3

Escape routes

When I was thirteen, Annette left home. She left school, got a job as an office junior, and moved out to share a flat with a friend. It was a big step for her, and where we lived it was unusual for a sixteen-year-old to leave home. I think she'd had enough of the poverty and violence of our home life, and had decided that she wanted something better. For her it was a good move: after years of acting as a substitute mother-figure to her eight younger brothers and sisters, she now had freedom, a home that stayed clean and tidy, and money to spend. For the rest of us it was devastating. I remember seeing her standing in the hallway with her bags, and knowing that our best support was gone.

I left school when I was fifteen. In those days it wasn't hard to get a job, and I went straight into a wool-blending factory. There were lots of other lads there, and we had a laugh. Our job was to fill the big wool hoppers. A huge plastic bag was fixed over a shaft about two feet square and eight feet deep, and wool came down a pipe and fell into it. We had to get a certain amount in each bag, so we sat above the opening and stamped the wool down with our feet. Once the bag was full, a huge suction tube at the bottom pulled it away and we fixed up a new one.

When a bag was nearly full, we sometimes jumped in and

trod on the wool with our whole weight, but one day I fell in (I was a skinny lad and easily fitted inside the shaft) and couldn't get back up. Luckily one of my mates was quick-thinking, and got a pole down for me to grab, and they pulled me out. Otherwise I could easily have been trapped inside the bale.

I stayed there about six months before moving to another job – this time in an upholstery factory. My Dad got me that job: he took me in to see the boss and asked if there were any jobs going. (I don't know what he knew about it, since he never had a job himself, but he was keen that we should all be earning.) I started as an apprentice cutter, earning £7 a week, which was a good wage in those days.

I worked with a senior cutter called Derek, and he taught me how to layer lots of fabrics together to cut the pieces for several suites at once, lay out the pattern on the fabric and chalk the outline. We used a big industrial saw to cut through the material, so it was quite a skilled job. I loved it. I was happy for the first time in my life. There was a good atmosphere in the factory and people were cheerful and friendly. It was much better than school, because I was learning and achieving something, and better than home because there were no rows or fighting. I had money in my pocket, and I was paying Mum for my board, which made me feel grown up.

I used to make a bit extra, too, because it was my job to do the dinner run for the ladies in the sewing room, taking their orders for food and going into the town centre to collect it. They were a motherly lot, all sitting in rows at their sewing machines, and they often used to tell me to keep the change. I also did a deal with the owner of one of the shops in town – I'd bring all their orders for pies or fish and chips to him, and in exchange he gave me a free meal. Good money and free food – it didn't get much better than that!

Then I got my first girlfriend, and I was even happier. Sally Johnson really was my first love. She was great – she saw me as the person I was inside, and didn't seem to notice the scars and disfigurement. I knew her from school (she was a year younger than me), but now we started dating. I often used to take the bus out to her house in Mytholmroyd, a couple of miles from where I lived in Hebden Bridge.

One Sunday night I was waiting at the bus stop to go home: I'd had a lovely evening with Sally, just talking and listening to music in her room – it was really romantic. Then my mate Stuart came up, waiting for the same bus back to Hebden Bridge. His evening had been very different from mine: he'd just been thrown out of a night club in the town. I wasn't surprised – Stuart was a big-built Scotsman with a reputation for being hard and quite stroppy. He claimed there hadn't been any fighting, just a noisy argument with a gang of lads from Todmorden, but the bouncers hadn't liked the shouting and ejected the lot of them. In those days there was a lot of gang warfare between the different areas around Halifax: Todmorden guys didn't go into Hebden Bridge and vice versa – but Mytholmroyd was neutral territory. I guess they'd all had a drink or two, some insults had been exchanged and things got out of hand.

When the bus came it was about half-past ten and the bottom deck was filled with pensioners going home from their evening's bingo. We paid and went upstairs, and sat in a seat opposite the top of the stairs – I was by the window and Stuart was by the aisle. At the next stop there seemed to be a long wait and a bit of a commotion downstairs, but we were chatting and didn't take much notice. Then a big crowd of lads came up, shouting and yelling, and went to sit at the back. Stuart glanced up and said to me in an undertone, "There could be a bit of trouble, Peter. They're the ones I was arguing with."

All of a sudden two or three lads jumped over the seats at the back and came forward up the bus. I felt a thump behind my head – a kick or a punch – which knocked me forward. Someone behind me was raining blows down on my back and head. I hunched up to protect myself and looked sideways to my right, and saw Stuart standing up and fighting his way back down the aisle, with four or five guys elbowing for room to get a punch at him.

Looking up was a mistake – another punch pushed me forward and I fell sideways, wedged in the space between our seat and the one in front. I put my hands up to protect my face. Suddenly all the lads fighting Stuart backed off, leaving one guy facing him. Stuart turned away and the guy pulled out a knife with a long blade, and stuck it straight into his back. He pulled the blade out, covered in blood, and more blood spurted out after it. Stuart collapsed forward over a seat.

I watched in horror as the guy with the knife turned round, spattered in Stuart's blood, and saw me cowering on the bus floor. I'll never forget his face – it was twisted with anger and hatred. He didn't know me, but he pointed at me and said, "You – yer bastard!" and raised his arm. For a split second I was convinced I was going to die, and I instinctively rolled to my left, raising my right arm over my head. Then he lunged downwards, plunging the knife into my upper arm and ripping it downwards. It felt like the heaviest punch you've ever had, but at least it was my arm and not my chest. I didn't feel any pain at first, just the blow and the sensation of tearing as the knife ripped through flesh and muscle.

The bloke backed away into the crowd of lads who were suddenly quiet. Then someone grabbed me by my hair and pulled me upright, and I saw with amazement that it was Stuart. "We've got to get off!" he hissed urgently, backing towards the stairs and dragging me by my hair.

Somehow we stumbled down the stairs, with Stuart shouting at the driver to stop and let us off. At the bottom, we clutched at the hand-rails to steady ourselves, and stood there swaying, covered in blood. Some of the women sitting at the front started screaming at the sight of us. The driver looked round.

"I can't put you off here," he said, "you'll bleed to death!" He was right – the bus was still in the countryside. At least it was only a few minutes into the town. I was wearing a leather jacket with tight cuffs, and I suddenly realized that my right sleeve was all puffed up, and blood was trickling down over my wrist. I opened the zip and pulled the jacket off, and blood poured out of the sleeve. The screaming from the women increased. I looked round hazily, and it seemed that all I could see were all these old faces with their mouths open in horror. At least no one had followed us downstairs.

A couple of minutes later the bus pulled into Hebden Bridge and the driver opened the doors. "I'll call the police from the next phone box," he said. We staggered off the bus and it drove off. I fell to the ground and lay there. I didn't care about anything any more – I just wanted to sleep. Across the road there was a taxi rank with a little office. I don't know where Stuart got his strength from – he had been stabbed too – but he managed to get over there and call for help. Then he ran out of steam and finally collapsed on the floor. Two of the drivers ran out and picked me up, carried me inside and put me on an old sofa.

After that everything's a blur. I must have lost a lot of blood. I heard sirens and saw flashing lights, and heard the paramedics calling me to stay awake, but I drifted away and the blackness closed in.

The next day I woke up in hospital. I was very woozy, and the light felt very bright. It was easier to keep my eyes closed. Gradually the events of the night before came back to me. How badly had I been hurt? As awareness returned, I realized that I couldn't feel my right hand. I could lift my left, however, and I raised it slowly under the stiff white sheet. I felt across my chest to where my right arm should be – nothing. My heart missed a beat. Had they amputated it? Then I opened my eyes and saw my own arm, heavily bandaged, held up in front of me in a complex traction arrangement, complete with drains and drips. I thought it must have been heavily anaesthetized, because I couldn't feel it at all.

For ages I drifted in and out of sleep, and every time I woke I went over what had happened. I kept seeing the guy's face as he stabbed me. And what about Stuart? I don't know how long it was before that question was answered, but one day I opened my eyes and saw Stuart in a wheelchair beside my bed. He had come to see how I was doing. Although he had received a stab wound to his body, he had actually been less seriously injured than me. He was allowed to go home after a few days. I was kept in for six weeks.

The problem was that as the knife went into my arm it had severed all the tendons. My whole arm felt dead. There was extensive nerve damage, and I was unable to move my wrist or fingers at all. Later on I found I was able to move my arm up and down and bend my elbow, but I had lost all the fine motor control. I could feel my fingers but not use them.

As soon as I recovered from the loss of blood, I had to have operations to replace the damaged tendons with plastic ones. The result was that as well as the collection of scars I already had from my burns, I now had some more from all the operations on my right arm.

Once I began to heal, it was back to the physiotherapy department. What a relief it was when I finally began to be able to move my fingers! I've got no fingers at all on my left hand, so losing my right was totally incapacitating. I had a cast on my arm for about a year after I was discharged, and continued to have physiotherapy on my hand. They nicknamed me "the Golfer" because they gave me a golf ball to squeeze, throw up in the air and catch. Over the next six months or so I slowly regained most of the movement, though I still have only about 80 per cent of the normal flexibility in my wrist.

Back at home I couldn't do anything for myself – the combination of the injuries to my right hand and the existing disability in my left meant that I was helpless. I lost my job immediately because I couldn't manipulate the patterns or the power cutters we used. I had to sign on for "the sick" – I was on incapacity benefit for about two years – so I could pay Mum for my board and lodging. She must have thought I was the unluckiest of all her children. After such a bad start in life, it seemed I was doing all right at last, and now here I was, injured yet again, and as dependent as a child.

In the long boring hours of the day, or when I lay awake at night, I used to think about the man who stabbed me. The only thing that felt really alive in me was the longing for revenge that burned in my heart. I used to imagine meeting him in a pub and following him into the toilet. I'd take a few of my mates and we'd beat him up. No, we wouldn't, we'd torture him first. We'd make him feel as bad as I did. We'd make sure he couldn't work, or cut up his own food. Then we'd beat him up some more. But we wouldn't kill him. Being dead was easy. Staying alive when your life had been taken away – that's what was hard.

It didn't help that he'd more or less got away with it. Somewhere along the bus route home he'd thrown the knife out of the window and it had never been recovered. The police took a statement from me in hospital, and the whole gang were arrested, and some of them were charged. The case went to Todmorden Magistrates' Court, and the guy turned up in a smart suit, said he was sorry, and blamed Stuart for starting the fight. He got twelve months on probation. In those days violence was routine in Todmorden and Hebden Bridge – they were rough areas. The magistrates were used to seeing glassings and stabbings. Nowadays the law is tougher on people who carry knives, but then it just rubbed salt in my wounds. Why should he get off so lightly when he'd ruined my life?

That's what it felt like. In hospital I'd been cocooned by the routine and the focus on my injuries, but once I left the ward, reality hit home. I felt like a lost cause: why me? What had I done to suffer all this? I had so little – why should what I had be taken away? Almost the only bit of me that was unharmed in the fire was my right hand and arm, and now they were gone. Why couldn't it have been my left arm, already damaged, that got wrecked?

Depression closed in. No matter where I looked, life seemed hopeless. I couldn't work. I didn't want to go out with my mates – I didn't have the money, and anyway people stared at my cast and bandages. I didn't want to meet anyone. Events had conspired to ruin my body: I was useless and the world seemed to be closed to me. I didn't have a place in ordinary life with normal people. I was lost, bewildered and angry. During the day I slept a lot, trying to shut out my awareness of everything.

I'd even lost my girlfriend. Sally visited me when I was in hospital, but after I came out I didn't see her so often. I didn't have the money for the bus, and when we did meet up I don't suppose I was very good company, morose and bitter as I was. Eventually she stopped coming. Then, one rare evening when I went into town, I saw her coming out of a pub with another bloke. They were laughing together. It wasn't the fact that she'd found someone else that hurt me, it was the way they seemed to be having a good time. I sat at the bus stop and cried. Why couldn't I ever have a laugh? What had I done that made my life such rubbish? And always the same question – why should everything happen to me? Those questions were to haunt me for years.

Being at home didn't help. The house was the same squalid chaos it had always been, and Mum and Dad were still fighting, screaming abuse at each other and occasionally coming to blows. We got kicked out of the house in Hebden Bridge, and moved to yet another council house in Mixenden, north-west of Halifax. I had a bit of money now: Dad had taken me to a solicitor and explained what had happened to me. He thought I should be entitled to some compensation through the Criminal Injuries Compensation Board. The solicitor agreed – in fact he was so sure of it that he gave us an advance of £1,000 on the spot. Dad went to the bank, cashed the cheque, and split it with me. I had £500 in my pocket, but it didn't last long. I started on a downward spiral of self-destruction, spending my money on anything that would help me escape from the depression. I was a young man who should have been having the time of my life. Instead I was stuck at home all day, totally dependent on Dad or anyone else who was around. I couldn't even get a drink of water for myself.

Mostly it wasn't water I wanted. Alcohol offered the fastest route out of my misery, and I took it. Mum and Dad were both drinkers, and there were always cans and bottles in the house – what was inside depended on how much money was about. When times were hard it was only cheap cider, which was the only thing I wouldn't touch. I'd been put off it as a lad: I smuggled a big bottle into a school party, and drank so much of it that I collapsed and was rushed into hospital. Having your stomach pumped is pretty traumatic when you're thirteen, and it put me off cider for life.

Still, there were plenty of other things to drink, and I tried most of them. Once my bandages were off, and I had a little movement back in my hand – enough to hold a glass, at any rate – I sometimes went out to the pub with my mates. They felt sorry for me, and they used to buy me drinks. After the first few, the pain was blunted: life looked rosier when viewed through the bottom of a glass.

The same went for drugs. It was easy to get soft drugs in the pubs in Halifax, and cannabis bought me a way out of depression for an hour or two. A few puffs, and a feeling of euphoria would envelop me. I thought it reminded me of what life used to be like, before I lost my job, my girl and my ability to live a normal life. It took my mind off my misery, and I felt less stressed out. I stopped worrying about the future (was I going to be on the dole for life?) and focused on how I felt at that moment. Unfortunately it didn't last long – but that just made me want to seek out the feeling again.

Of course, my dole money wouldn't pay for much in the way of drink and drugs. I needed more. Fortunately I thought I knew another way to get money – a way that gave me another brief diversion from my situation. Dad had shown me that. I remember once when I was twelve, sitting in the pub with Dad. He was over by the bar with his mates, drinking, and I suppose I must have been in the side-room where kids were allowed, with a bag of crisps to keep me quiet. He came over and pushed a bundle of fivers into my hand, along with a crumpled piece of paper.

"Go round the betting office, Peter," he said. "Give this to Harry – he's the man behind the counter. Tell him it's from me."

I knew about the betting office – I'd waited outside it often enough – but I'd never been inside it before. I went round there, full of importance, with what seemed like a huge wad of money stuffed deep in my trouser pocket. The shop was crowded with men, and the air was filled with cigarette smoke. No one paid any attention to me as I pushed my way towards the counter. They were all listening to a voice coming from a speaker high up on the wall. The man's voice got more and more excited as the race came to a climax: by the end he was screaming out the commentary, and I could hardly understand him. The atmosphere was electric. A couple of the men shouted wildly and threw their arms in the air, but the others seemed to wilt with disappointment. Conversations broke out all over the room, and men dropped their betting slips on the floor, while the happy few shouldered their way to the counter to collect their winnings.

I waited till they were served, then I went to the counter and pushed my dirty bit of paper across it. Harry looked down at me. His glasses were perched on the bridge of his nose.

"Does your Dad know you're here, lad?" he asked.

"Course he does," I said, trying to act casual. "He told me to give you this, from him." I pulled the notes from my pocket and handed them over.

Harry grunted when he saw the money. Then he produced a betting slip, wrote on it, and stamped it with a thud. He pushed it back across the counter.

"You tell your Dad that next time he wants a bet, he'd better bring it in himself. Understand, boy?"

I swallowed. I wasn't sure why he sounded so angry. I took a deep breath of smoky air and said, "OK, Harry." I felt a certain satisfaction about me and Harry being on first-name terms.

Back in the pub, I gave Dad the betting slip.

"Any trouble putting it on?" he asked.

"No, Dad. It was fine," I said. I felt very grown up, being in the pub with Dad, and I wasn't going to spoil it by telling him what Harry said.

"Good boy. OK, now shut up." The bar had gone quiet, and all the men in there had turned towards the big wall-mounted TV in the corner. It was just like it had been in the betting shop – everyone focused on the race, the excitement, the tension, the rising inflection of the commentator's voice. I found myself holding my breath as Dad's horse took the lead. I'd never seen my Dad so excited: he was grinning from ear to ear, and his fist was clenched round the betting slip that was about to be worth a fortune. Then just as the horse cleared the final jump it seemed to stumble. Its head went down, the front legs buckled and horse and jockey tumbled in a muddle of legs and mud. The other horses leapt clear of them and passed them. Dad's face fell. His whole body sagged, and he sat back down on his bar stool like a puppet whose strings had been cut. It was all over.

I never learned the obvious lesson – that the money had been lost in a moment. What I remembered from that day was only the good feelings: the camaraderie in the bar, my Dad's excitement, how good it was to do something for him that made him happy, and the possibility that you could win big money. So now, when the rest of my life had brought me low, I recaptured those good feelings by making my way back to the betting shop and putting on bets of my own. Soon it was my first port of call after getting my dole money, and I had added another addiction to the drink and drugs. Those three things gave a sort of structure to my shapeless days: have a drink, put on a bet, then score some drugs with any money that was left, to take away the sting of the disappointment. I was hiding from real life, but these activities gave me the illusion that I was living again, feeling better, even if it was only for a short while.

It brought me closer to Dad, as well. I was still only seventeen or so, and it felt good to go out drinking with him, or to the betting shop, or playing cards. He used to drink in a working-men's club in Mixenden, and there was a big table in the hall where men played cards – mostly three-card brag, with lots of cash in the pot, sometimes as much as £200. We never seemed to win, but the hope was always there, and there was drink and a convivial atmosphere. I felt like a man for once.

I started dating a girl called Lynne. Her parents had split up, and her mum was planning to move to Bristol with Trevor, her boyfriend, to manage a pub. Lynne was going with them to live in the flat above the pub, and she asked me if I'd like to come too. I decided I would – after all, I didn't have a job, and I could draw the dole as easily down south as at home. I'd never been so far from Halifax, but suddenly it seemed like another possible escape route. I could get away from home, be independent for

45

once. I went with them, got myself a room in a house nearby and settled in. Maybe my life was looking up again.

I didn't do so much gambling in Bristol, but I still drank a lot. Lynne was living over a pub, after all, and I could easily hang out there when she was working in the bar. The problem in Bristol was drugs. It was a more affluent area than the places I was used to: no council estates with people living on the dole, but students and people with jobs and more money. Consequently the drugs were harder.

One night a couple of weeks after I'd moved in, the guy upstairs knocked on my door and asked me if I wanted to go to a party. This was more like it – the start of a social life! I made some excuse to Lynne and got ready. One useful thing I had done with my compensation money was to buy some decent clothes, so I dressed up the way I would if I was going for a night out in Halifax: sharp suit, clean shirt and tie. I looked at my reflection in the mirror with satisfaction. I looked OK, and my self-esteem took a step up.

When the bloke knocked on my door later on, I was amazed to see that he was wearing a scruffy duffle coat, a Led Zeppelin tee-shirt and jeans with holes in. "Well, he's not going to pull tonight, looking like that," I thought. We went out to Clifton, the student area, and knocked at the door of a big four-storey town house. Loud music was spilling out onto the street, and the windows were practically shaking to the beat. Cars were parked all over the pavement. I began to realize that the night life in Clifton was a bit different from Halifax.

A girl with dishevelled blonde hair let us in, and we went into a crowded room full of smoke. I reckon you could have got high just breathing in the air. The circle of sofas and armchairs was full of young people dressed casually, in jeans and tee-shirts. I could see I was going to stick out like a sore thumb, so I took off my jacket and tie and opened a few buttons on my shirt. Then I sat on the arm of a sofa and tried to look relaxed. I'd never seen anything like it. I'd only been there a couple of minutes when the guy next to me on the sofa said, "Have some of this, man," and offered me a spliff. I had four or five puffs and passed it on – I knew it was a joint of some kind but it was much stronger than anything I'd ever tried before. A minute or two later I fell off the arm of the chair and crawled across the floor to the wall. I spent most of the night there, sitting in one place, leaning against the wall, completely out of my head. I don't know how I got home, but I was a complete wreck.

It must have been either crack cocaine or heroin – it certainly wasn't cannabis. At any rate, I liked it. When I was crawling across the floor, I didn't feel like unlucky Peter with his disabilities. I thought I was a lion, strong and powerful, crossing the plains where I was king. It had to be an improvement on the reality.

My time in Bristol didn't last long – maybe six months. Lynne's mum and Trevor moved on to another pub, and Lynne was missing home, so she and I went back north. I moved back in with my parents for a while, and then got myself a flat. I managed to get a job, too, in an engineering works in Sowerby Bridge, which made specialist parts for tractors. It wasn't a skilled job: I was a fettler – I had to prepare lumps of metal for the machine operators. I had a hammer in my right hand and a glove on my left to hold the chunk of metal as it came from the kiln (I never let on how hard it was for me to do so, especially when the piece was large), and I knocked off any sharp edges. I was relieved that I had regained enough control of my hands to do the job.

By this time the full amount of my compensation money had come through – it amounted to £4,000 – so I put down a deposit on a house, and got a mortgage with Lynne, and we moved in together. It lasted about a year before I discovered that she was having an affair. We had a big row and she moved out, and I went on living there alone for another six months or so until the house was sold. I'm not sure I was even that badly hurt when things turned out the way they did. I had thought I loved Lynne, and I had thought my life was looking up – but I'd been knocked back so many times before, it seemed almost inevitable that it would all fall apart eventually. It was almost a sort of relief when it did. I had learned to hold back on the euphoria when things were going well, because I always expected them to end in rejection and disaster.

After that I drifted. I shared a flat with another lad, then lived alone; I changed jobs and worked as a lathe turner with another engineering firm. I made friends, so I had people to drink with. I was living a lad's life, drinking, womanizing, working all week to earn the money, then going to clubs at weekends for drinking sessions (mostly lager and rum), and taking drugs (mostly cannabis and speed). I was earning decent money, so I could afford to keep up with the lifestyle. From time to time I went back to gambling, because it added a spice of excitement to the mundane life I was living otherwise – getting up, going to work, out to the pub, going home and sleeping. I had one or two girlfriends, but no relationships came to anything – possibly because I couldn't really focus on anyone else, or think about anything other than how to have a good time, in order to shut out the darkness which always lay in wait for me.

The rest of my twenties went by in a blur. There was a misery deep down inside me, and I sought solace and escape through drink and drugs. Sadly, they never seemed to work.

Chapter 4

Into the dungeon

Looking back, it seems amazing that I kept going for as long as I did. It wasn't just my self-destructive lifestyle – things happened to me that never seemed to happen to anyone else. It really did feel as if someone or something was determined to finish me off.

I was twenty-three when the next disaster caught up with me. I'd been out for the evening with my brother John and our friend Paul. Paul was a bit of a problem. He was fine when he was sober, but he was aggressive when he was drunk, and that night he'd had a few. I hadn't drunk much for once, because I'd been playing snooker for money, and I knew I needed a good head for that. (Even so, I hadn't made much money. My Dad was a much better player, because being unemployed, he always had plenty of time to practise.)

Anyway, when we came out of the snooker hall we decided to get a taxi, but the taxi driver refused to take Paul: he could see how drunk he was, and didn't want him throwing up in his cab. Paul had already started shouting at him, and I thought, "I'm having nothing to do with this." I could see it was going to end in a fight, so I walked off up the road.

I got as far as the T-junction at the top of the town when I heard the other two running up the street behind me. I looked to my right and saw two bright lights coming towards me, and heard an engine roaring – and then nothing.

I woke up in hospital. Again. I knew I'd been run over, but I couldn't put together the jigsaw of what had happened. I remember a couple of policemen coming to my bedside to try to take a statement, but I couldn't help them. I literally didn't know what had hit me.

Later on, John told me what had happened. As I'd predicted, Paul ended up punching the taxi driver, and the pair of them ran away up the road after me. The man jumped in his taxi and drove off, but he drove round three sides of the square, and was coming along the road to my right just as I was crossing. When the car hit me I was thrown high in the air and landed on my head. The taxi swerved past me and roared off into the distance, and John and Paul ran over to where I lay in the road. They thought I was dead – I was unconscious and blood was trickling out of my mouth. Luckily for me, a passing police patrol gave me first aid and called an ambulance. They probably saved my life.

I had a fractured skull, severe bruising to my back, and a broken collar bone and ribs. The worst injury, though, was a broken femur. I had to have a pin inserted in my thigh – another scar to match all the rest. I have a scar across the top of my head, too, from the skull fracture. There was a long period when the doctors feared that I might have brain damage, and I believe that there was some real change in my brain function: I developed a stammer, and sometimes I struggled to find the right words. I certainly think more slowly than I used to.

When I finally came out of hospital the owner of the taxi rank came to see me, and told me that he had sacked the driver.

He knew perfectly well who was responsible for the hit-and-run accident, but no charges were ever brought. I was filled with a burning sense of injustice. The police knew the facts: Paul and John had been charged with the assault on the taxi driver, gone to court and been fined, but there was no mention of what happened to me. I wondered sometimes if it was because our family was so well known to the police. Between us we'd been arrested for shoplifting, burglary and assault, as well as all the trouble we'd caused the council. In any case, it increased my resentment of the police and the whole criminal justice system. It took me years to recover from my injuries, but I didn't think I'd ever get over the injustice of it.

I came out of hospital in a wheelchair, and then I was on crutches for three months. At least it forced me off the drugs and gambling, because I couldn't get around easily to the betting shop or the drug dealers. I kept drinking, though – I could always find a member of the family happy to wheel me to the pub. I'd gone home to Mum yet again, and she looked after me. History repeating itself. I was in despair, wondering whether I would ever get out of this cycle of injury and dependence. One thing was different: Mum got fed up with me sitting around moaning, and she bought me a CB radio. It was the first time I'd ever had a hobby, and it took my mind off things a bit. Also, my relationship with Mum was better these days. When I was about sixteen she stopped hitting me. I suppose I was getting too big and strong. Nowadays she wasn't so irritable, though that may have been because she wasn't living with Dad and coping with so many young kids. Still, we never talked about the past, and the business of me getting burned as a baby was never mentioned. Perhaps looking after me each time I got injured helped her to deal with her guilt about that. She never complained about the fact that I was back at home at the age of twenty-four, being cared for like a child yet again.

So I was back again in the routine of recovery and building up my strength. The body has amazing powers of recuperation, but the mind and spirit are not always so resilient. I had developed quite a fatalistic attitude to life, born of experience: every time I climbed back up, something happened to knock me down again. Still, even though I had come to expect disaster lurking around the corner, it never stopped me from trying to rebuild my life.

As soon as I was well enough, I left – not just Mum's house, but Halifax. One of my mates suggested trying our luck in London, and that sounded exciting. We knew there was always work available on building sites, so off we went. My mate didn't like it much and came back home, but I got a room in a scruffy bed-and-breakfast place in Paddington and a job as a labourer. The work was hard but it paid well, and in London there were plenty of pubs and plenty of drug dealers, so I reckoned I was OK.

I spent most of my money on drugs. You could get anything, and I tried most things: cannabis, speed (amphetamines) and acid. The one thing I never tried was heroin, though I had been thinking about it. One day I had a bad experience. I was living in a "hotel" (actually just a house full of individually let rooms) and I went to buy some drugs from the guy who lived on the floor below. There was no answer when I knocked, but the door was ajar, so I pushed it open. It was a big room with two beds in it, a double and a single. A couple were lying on the double bed, still and silent. There was blood everywhere, on their arms and sprayed up the walls. It looked as though someone had been killed there. The girl was about seventeen, and she was as pale as death. Her eyes were open and bulging, and she had a needle still hanging out of her arm.

I stood there and gaped at them in shock. "That's what heroin does to you," I thought, and I turned and ran back upstairs. I never found out if they were dead or still alive.

I was lonely in London. I felt a long way from home, even though I'd never been especially close to my family. I had mates at work, and people I met in the pub, but I didn't have any close friends, and no girlfriends. That's when I started going to prostitutes. For a bit of cash you could buy the illusion of being close to someone, but as soon as it was over I always hated myself for doing it – I'd go home and feel filthy.

Eventually all these bad feelings got on top of me, and I decided to try my luck somewhere else. Maybe it was just London that was so impersonal. Perhaps in a smaller city I might feel more connected to people. I moved to Bournemouth, and got more building-site work, but of course life was what I made of it, and I only knew a few ways of enjoying myself: drink, drugs and gambling. I hardly ever gambled when I had money coming in – it was always being hard up that made me susceptible to the lure of easy money. So I went back to working all week, and spending my pay packet at the weekend on beer and cannabis.

In Bournemouth I had another narrow escape from death. I was working as a hoist operator on an eight-storey building.

One Saturday morning I was going up in the hoist – a sort of cage in a hydraulic lift on the side of the building. Below me a bloke was preparing to send some scaffolding poles up to the top of the building, and he was strapping them together with a chain attached to the crane. I looked out and saw the poles catching me up and overtaking the hoist. For some reason I felt uneasy, and then suddenly I panicked, stopped the lift, and pressed the "down" button. At the bottom I got out and walked away. I was only about ten feet away when I heard a crash. One scaffolding pole had escaped from the bundle and came down like an arrow. It went straight through the hoist cage and stuck deep in the ground. If I had been inside, it would have gone right through me.

At least it was a change from my usual luck. That made me feel quite cheerful for a while, but it didn't last long. A few months later the contracts manager called me into his office.

"Sit down, Peter," he said. "I've got your brother on the phone."

It was John. "Bad news, Peter," he said. "It's Dad. He's committed suicide."

I couldn't believe it. It turned out that he had been prescribed Valium for depression, but he'd taken an overdose. Combined with all the alcohol in his bloodstream, it was enough to kill him. John had gone round to see him and couldn't get an answer when he knocked at the door, so he went round the back and climbed in through the window. When he found Dad on the bed he called an ambulance, but the paramedics said he was already dead.

John seemed to want to tell me every detail, as though

by going over and over it he could make himself believe it. Apparently the day before he died, Dad had done something very out of character – he'd gone to a church and talked to a priest. He must have been thinking about suicide.

I got on the train back to Halifax and went straight round to Mum's. All the family had gathered there, looking stunned. None of us could get our heads round it. We couldn't understand why Dad had finally got so depressed that he wanted to take his own life. I went to the undertaker's to see his body, as if by looking at him I could make myself believe that he was really dead, but all I could remember was Dad when he'd been drinking or gambling, cheering a horse on, or flashing his money about in the pub and buying me drinks.

He was buried in Copley, where he grew up, because we knew he had fond memories of living there. Dad's death left a deep hole in our family. We all felt guilty: could we have done anything? Would it have been different if we'd been there, visited him more often, taken him out for a drink? We were all devastated in our different ways, but maybe June and Adrian most of all. After Mum had moved out and the rest of us had left, they had stayed at home in Mixenden and tried to look after Dad.

David had left home at fifteen to move in with his girlfriend. They had two kids and lived just round the corner from Dad. Susan got married when she was sixteen, and so did John. Tony, Jim and I were single but living in different places, wherever we found work. I didn't usually see much of the rest of the family, though they were all living in the same area, and had similar lifestyles to mine. The only exception was Annette. She was married to a man who owned a butcher's shop, and seemed to be living a quiet and prosperous life with their children. I rather envied her – of all of us, she seemed to have broken out of the circle of chaos and destruction that was all our childhood had prepared us for.

Dad's death sent me down into a really deep depression. Whenever I thought about him dying alone in that cold flat, I felt guilty. I knew the sort of life he'd lived, spending most of his time either drunk or suffering from the resulting hangover. His only pleasure was gambling, but even that wasn't exactly enjoyable, because he mostly lost. His only real friend was Jeff the bookie, who used to take him out and buy him beer. But a day out with Jeff wasn't much fun because it involved betting heavily – he might act like a mate but he always ended up taking all your money, and Dad would come home skint, just marking time till the next dole day. It was a miserable existence.

What I never managed to do was see the parallels between Dad's life and mine – the loneliness, the failed relationships, the drink and the gambling. I didn't compare myself with him because I was young and he seemed old to me. I didn't look ahead and see what I might become.

I drifted on, restless and miserable, but powerless to make any changes to my world. I moved to Brighton briefly, but found it no better, and returned to Halifax where at least my family knew me. This time I got a room in a boarding house in Mixenden, which by coincidence turned out to be the old children's home I'd spent time in as a child – I was even in the same room that had been my bedroom. It only confirmed to me that I was going round and round in a groove, with no escape. I was unemployed again, so I did a bit of shoplifting. I needed something to sell to get money for drink, drugs and gambling.

At this time I was probably at the worst stage of my drug addiction, and I was desperate for cash so I could meet my constant need for amphetamines just to keep going. I started dealing, travelling to Liverpool to buy drugs and selling them in the pubs and clubs nearer home. I never got caught, and it seemed to be easy money: I could buy the gear for £300 and sell it for £600 or £700. I never thought about the people I was entrapping in the same downward spiral as my own. It was a horrible lifestyle, constantly either desperate for drugs or high on them, watching anxiously for the police and in fear of being arrested or worse.

One day I went into a house with £400 in my pocket to buy speed. The guy I was buying from opened a drawer, and alongside the gear in packets lay a revolver. It was a shock. You see guns in American films, but in those days you didn't expect to see one in a back street in England. I suddenly realized how easy it would be for him to shoot me, pocket the money, and disappear. Who would know what happened to me?

I longed to get out of the miserable and dangerous rut I was living in, but I didn't know how. It was the only way of life I knew.

When I was twenty-seven, the rollercoaster of my life started uphill once more. I met a girl called Karen in a club. She'd just come out of a relationship and was smarting from the messy break-up. We just clicked, and she was good for me: she had a job and a car, so she could drive me around and take me out. She lifted me out of my misery, and there seemed to be some point to my life again.

When she told me she was pregnant, it was a massive shock, but also exciting. Out of all the chaos and tragedy of my life so far, maybe this really was a new beginning. The idea of a baby kick-started me into action, and made me want to get my life in order. Karen worked as a shop assistant in a jeweller's; I got a job in an engineering works, and with my overtime we were making good money. We bought a three-bedroom terraced house in Siddal, and set up home.

When our baby son was born, I was on Cloud Nine. I walked home from the hospital in a haze of happiness. My life was worth something: I was a dad! We called him Peter Edward, and the fact that he had my name confirmed my link with him. I doted on him. For a while everything was wonderful.

Sadly, I couldn't keep it up. A life of emotional deprivation, disaster and depression doesn't equip you to be a good father. Even my love for our son wasn't powerful enough to break the chains of my old lifestyle. Habits and addictions aren't easy to overcome just like that, without help. Having a crying baby at home wasn't easy, either, and I soon ran away, back to the drink and the drugs. A bit of me despised myself – Karen was at home with him all day, and when I got home from work I'd eat and then go out again and leave her to it.

Of course, to everyone else I appeared to be happy and in control of my life: I would never admit my problems, no matter how much chaos was going on inside. When I was in the pub with my mates I was always cheerful; I'd learned that from my Dad. He was a fighter who always acted tough. You had to keep up that image. It was weak to show emotion or let anyone see the cracks in your armour. My armour was almost all cracks.

Karen and I had only been together for two years when our relationship started to go downhill badly. She knew I was drinking again, but she didn't know about the drugs or the gambling. We'd put aside the housekeeping money each week, but I kept most of my pay packet for myself – I had plenty of things to spend it on. I used to play cards for big pots of money, though I didn't often win. The occasional drug deal kept me in pocket.

Neither of us knew how to build a strong relationship based on fidelity and trust, and we both had affairs. In the end Karen walked out, taking Peter Edward with her, and went back to live with her mum a few streets away. I should have seen it coming, but I felt as if someone had torpedoed the fragile ship of my life, and I was sinking. It's hard to describe my state of mind at that time – I was at an all-time low. I lost my job, because I was too depressed to get up in the morning and go to work, and when I did go in I was generally hungover. Within a couple of months I had sold all the stuff of value in the house (the settee, the TV and the stereo) to get money for drugs. I found myself roaming round the empty rooms, staring out of the windows in despair.

The only thing that enabled me to get out of bed each morning was the promise of the cocktail of drink and drugs waiting for me. Christmas was coming, and the bright lights in the shops and the people choosing gifts drove me deeper into despair. Everyone else had friends and families, and I had nothing. Everything I did get, I destroyed.

Scenes came and went in my mind: the years of pain in my childhood, struggling to learn to walk on burned feet; the vicious look on the face of the attacker who stabbed me; the dazzling lights of the car that mowed me down in the hit-and-run accident; the face of the dead heroin addict with the needle hanging from her arm; my Dad lying cold in his coffin. Perhaps the only way to end my years of pain was to take my own life, like Dad. How could I do it? One day I went to North Bridge and looked over it at the concrete roadway nearly eighty feet below. Was it a big enough drop to kill me? Perhaps if I had enough to drink first, I'd be able to do it. It was a thought – perhaps, even, a hope. I had had enough of this life.

On the last Sunday of my life, I got up and looked in the mirror. My face was thin and covered in stubble, my eyes sunken and bloodshot. I looked like an old man, broken in body, mind and spirit. My head was in turmoil, as if a battle was going on inside me. One minute I would think, "You'll be OK. Go out tonight, meet some mates, score some drugs. Forget it all." Then I'd hear another voice, saying, "Look at yourself, look at what you've done. You've driven everyone away. Your life's over anyway. May as well finish it."

In desperation I went out, slouching through the streets with my hands deep in my pockets. I saw a guy I knew coming towards me.

"All right, Peter? How's it going?" he asked.

I didn't answer. I didn't even look up at him. I just walked on. I felt like a dead man already.

I hadn't really made up my mind what I was going to do, but I found myself heading towards the bridge again. On the way I passed a church, and something about it drew me like a magnet. The churchyard was surrounded by black railings, and on impulse I tried the gate. It opened and I walked up the path, but the door was locked. It felt like the last straw.

"What am I doing?" I asked myself. "Standing in the porch of an old church, crying because the doors are locked and I can't get in."

I suppose the morning service was over and everyone had gone home. I wasn't thinking about God, or what I would have done if the church had been open. Perhaps I thought there might be someone there who would talk to me. Perhaps I was thinking about my Dad, who went to a church the day before he committed suicide. I was following in his footsteps now, all right.

It was a cold, lonely walk to North Bridge. The road was lined with factories, closed for the weekend, and there were hardly any cars about and no one else on foot. I might have been the last man in the world. By now I was numb with cold and misery. I stood in the middle of the bridge and looked down. I could climb over the railing and let myself drop – and then it would all be over. No more pain, no more loneliness, no more spoiling and destruction and guilt. I could let myself fall down, down onto the brutal concrete, and it would finish what I'd started. The end of a wasted life.

I grasped the iron parapet with both hands, trying to summon up the energy to climb over. Damn! I didn't even have the guts to jump. I took a deep breath, willing myself to move, to end it once and for all. Then out of the corner of my eye I glimpsed a feeble light. There was a block of flats a couple of hundred yards away – the flats where my Mum lived, on the fifth floor. It was morning, but one flat had a light on, a pinprick of yellow in the grey, overcast daylight. I counted the windows. It was my Mum's flat. All of a sudden I found myself turning towards the light. Dying could wait. Perhaps I'd go and see Mum first.

Chapter 5

Out of the
darkness

Just the fact that I even thought of going to Mum's flat tells you how much our relationship had changed. In some ways, Dad's death had done what he never did in life: bring the family together. We were never going to be close, but I think on that day when we all gathered for his funeral, we looked around and realized that having one another – and Mum – did mean something.

Nowadays Mum's flat had become something of a place of refuge for all of us when things went wrong. Her health wasn't so good these days – she'd been having some sort of heart trouble – but she kept cheerful and she always seemed pleased to see us. Mum wasn't one for hugging, and she didn't ask questions or offer advice. But she listened, and fed us and made cups of tea, and generally made us feel that she cared about us. It was a feeling I desperately needed that day.

I went up in the lift. Thank goodness it was working, because I didn't think I'd have the strength to climb five flights of stairs. I wasn't thinking about anything much, but as the doors opened and I stepped out, I found myself panicking in case she wasn't in. I'd seen a light in her window – but what if she'd gone out and left it on? What if I stood knocking at her front door the way I had at that church, and found it locked against me? It would be just like my luck. I lifted the knocker and let it bang down. I was ready just to turn away, but the door opened, and there stood Mum, in her flowery pinny just the same as always. Her smile faded as she took in my appearance: grubby, crumpled clothes, sunken, bloodshot eyes and a week's stubble. I walked straight past her into her little living-room and collapsed into an armchair, bending forward with my head in my hands. Tears ran through my fingers. I couldn't stop crying.

"It's over, Mum," I sobbed. "I can't go on. I've ruined my life. Everything's gone. It's a mess."

Mum stood looking at me in horror. She'd never seen me like this. Through all the years of depression and injury and pain, I'd never opened up to anyone about how I had felt – I'd kept it all hidden behind my pride, a cheery smile and being ready to buy the next round. Now all my defences were down. I looked up at her.

"Everything's gone," I said again. "They've taken Peter Edward. I'll never see him again. I've sold all the furniture. I've got nothing. No one."

Mum didn't know what to say, so she stalled for time.

"Cup of tea, Peter?" she asked. I heard the kettle clank on top of the enamel gas stove, the scratch of a match, the hiss of gas and the roar as it ignited. I knew she'd use the same match to light her fag. I sat staring at nothing till she came back, then I found myself with a mug of tea in one hand and a cigarette in the other.

Then she said, "I know, I'll ring our Annette." She picked up the phone.

I took a swig of tea. I couldn't remember when I last had a hot drink. I wasn't listening to Mum's conversation; I was eaten up with anguish and fear and despair. It was as if the real world outside my head hardly existed.

Then Mum took the mug out of my hand and gave me the phone.

"It's Annette, Peter. She wants to talk to you."

I made myself focus on Annette's voice coming over the phone. "Peter? You all right?"

"It's no use, Annette," I said. "I've messed everything up. I can't keep out of the bookie's, I need drugs all the time – I can't see a way out."

Annette didn't hesitate. She didn't skirt round it or sympathize, and what she said next blew me away.

"Look, Peter, eight weeks ago I became a Christian. My life was in a mess too, and the reason was sin. If you've messed up it's because of sin, and only God can deal with that. God can give you a brand-new life."

She didn't spout theology at me, she didn't try to offer any explanation – she just told me how it was, how she saw it, and it was like somebody throwing open the curtains and letting the daylight into my head. Light just streamed in – I could almost see it.

Suddenly I felt as if I had the answer to all the problems in my life.

"You're right, Annette! That's it! What do I have to do?"

I didn't know, then, that I was echoing the cry of sinners through the ages: "What must I do to be saved?" And Annette, the brand-new baby Christian who was right at the start of her own new life, said the one thing she knew for sure in her heart: "You have to give your life to Jesus."

At that moment I was in the grip of some powerful emotions. My dark despair was being torn aside by a shaft of bright hope, and I had a vision. I looked up and seemed to see a man standing in front of me. He was quite ordinary-looking, with brown hair and a beard, but he was dressed in a long white robe and he was holding his hands out to me.

I was gobsmacked – it was such a weird experience. I was in my Mum's front room, I was on the phone to my sister, and yet I felt as if I was looking into another world. He said, "Come to me, and I will give you rest."

I dropped the phone and fell forward out of the chair onto my knees; when I looked up again, through my tears, I could only see my Mum, hurrying over to me.

I picked up the phone and said, "Annette, you won't believe this. I've just seen Jesus."

There was a moment's pause, then she said, "Stay there, I'm coming over."

I handed the phone back to Mum and sat back in the chair. I think I was smiling – for the first time for weeks. It felt as if the sun had come out, and I was bathed in warmth and brightness. My heart had lifted and I didn't know why. What had just happened? Why had my pain and misery receded? Why did I suddenly feel calm and peaceful? All these questions had to wait till Annette arrived. I knew something different had happened, but I didn't have the words to explain it.

I understand it all so much better now. At that moment when Annette told me I had to give my life to Jesus, my heart said "Yes!" I didn't know fully what it meant, I didn't know what the implications were, but I knew she was offering me a lifeline and my spirit leapt up and grabbed it. My life depended on it.

That was the moment when I moved from death to life, from dangling over the abyss – the death I'd been looking down on from North Bridge – to setting my feet on the firm rock, a secure place to stand. "For the word of God is living and active ... it penetrates even to dividing soul and spirit" (Hebrews 4:12). I believe in that moment I was pierced and saved. I wonder if I'm the only person to give their life to Jesus with a phone in one hand and a fag in the other.

I sat there in a kind of dream. Mum was pottering about in the kitchen, but she didn't disturb me or ask what was going on. It seemed like only a few minutes had passed before she was opening the door again and Annette came in – my big sister who had always looked after me. She'd just done the biggest thing anyone can do for someone else: show them the door to eternal life.

She took off her coat and came over and sat down. Even though I was still sitting there stunned and tear-stained, I could sense something different about her. She looked happy, full of some deep joy that buoyed her up. There was an air of calm and contentment about her that made me even more aware of the chaos in my own heart.

"Can I pray for you?" she asked. I nodded. I didn't even stop to think how odd it was for her to be saying that. We'd never thought much about religion in our family. Now it seemed the most important thing in the world. Annette didn't go on about her faith, and she didn't deliver a ten-ton message or try to explain everything at once. She just led me in the Sinner's Prayer:

"Father, I know I've made a mess of things. I know my sins have separated me from you. I'm truly sorry. I want to turn away from my sinful life and come to you. I believe that your Son Jesus Christ died to save me from my sins, that he is alive today and hears my prayer. I ask Jesus to come into my life as Lord, to reign in my heart for ever. Please send your Holy Spirit to show me the way to obey you and do your will. Amen."

I whispered "Amen" after her. I never meant anything so strongly in my life. I was clinging on to those promises of a new way of living.

Mum and Annette must have had a chat, because the next thing was that we were all getting into Annette's car and driving to her house in Buttershaw. She got us something to eat, and suggested that we should all go to the evening service at her church. Mum was a bit bemused, but she was relieved to see me looking less shattered, so she agreed.

I don't know what I'd been expecting – probably a dull service with unintelligible hymns, like a school assembly – but it was nothing like that. I sat in a pew with Mum and Annette and looked around. Everyone seemed so cheerful and friendly. And the worship songs were lively, with good tunes and words that spoke to me – about Jesus being our Saviour, about God loving us – me, as a person.

I felt as though I'd been living my life in a dark dungeon, and Annette had opened a door and let the light in. And now I was slowly climbing the cellar steps, one at a time, towards freedom. Sitting in church with my Mum and my sister, listening to the music, I went up another step away from the darkness.

Then the Pastor got up and preached a message of salvation. He explained how I could come into a relationship with God through Jesus Christ, and he read some things from the Bible. Some of the verses stuck in my head:

"For God so loved the world that he gave his one and only Son, that whoever believes in him shall not perish but have eternal life" (John 3:16). "For all have sinned and fall short of the glory of God" (Romans 3:23). "If we confess our sins, he is faithful and just and will forgive us our sins and purify us from all unrighteousness" (1 John 1:9).

I didn't need convincing that I was a sinner. I've met some people who hide behind "I don't do any harm, I never killed anyone, so I'm OK." That wasn't for me. I knew instinctively that you can't pigeonhole sin: I'd done so many things I was ashamed of, and my heart was so full of bitterness and anger that it answered the charge at once. I was guilty. I felt as if I was waving a white flag and saying "I surrender."

Then the Pastor made the altar call: "If you want to give your life to Jesus, come to the front of the church and I'll pray with you." I knew he was talking to me.

Some music started – they were playing "Amazing Grace". I knew the words because a version had been in the charts in the 1970s, and they spoke to me as powerfully as the scriptures had:

Amazing grace, how sweet the sound
That saved a wretch like me.

I once was lost, but now I'm found;
Was blind, but now I see.

I turned to Mum and Annette with tears streaming down my face and put my arms round them both. Then, without a word, I got up and made my way down the aisle to the front of the church. It didn't matter to me that no one else got up, that I was the only person to go forward. I didn't care what anyone else thought of me.

I knelt down at the altar rail and the Pastor knelt beside me and put his arm round me.

"What do you want to do?" he asked quietly.

"I want to give my life to Jesus," I said. He led me in a prayer like the one Annette had prayed that afternoon, and I repeated the words after him. Then the Pastor thanked God that I had been born again into eternal life. We both stood up, and the Pastor said, "Welcome to the family of God."

I turned to walk back to my seat in a daze. Going forward, I had been drawn to the altar, but I still felt as if I was carrying a sack of coal, the weight of all my failures and sins. Walking back down the aisle I felt free, released: I had left my burden behind. Another step up from that dungeon.

When the service was over, two men came up and introduced themselves. We sat and chatted for a while, and they gave me a leaflet with the words of that prayer printed out, and some tips about reading the Bible and going to church. Then they prayed for me, too, asking God to guide me in my new life and fill me with the Holy Spirit. I felt so blessed by that prayer. I breathed in and seemed to be filled with new life and energy. I believe I was filled with the Holy Spirit at that moment. It was another gift from God, and I felt lifted up another step.

We walked back to Annette's house and then she drove us back to Mum's. I was quiet on the drive home, trying to take in what had happened. What an amazing day it had been! From the moment Annette had spoken to me on the phone, I had been changing. At every stage, I felt God had been lifting me, one step at a time, up out of the dungeon I had built for myself. The spirit of despair had been driven out of me and replaced with encouragement and strength.

Mum had made up a bed in the spare room, so I went in there and knelt by the bed to pray my first independent prayer:

"Dear Lord," I said, "for the past thirty years I've made a complete mess of my life. I want to surrender my life to you, and give you whatever years I have left. In Jesus' name. Amen."

Then I got into bed and slept like a baby.

When I opened my eyes the next morning I wondered if I would still feel different – but I did. For a start, I didn't have a hangover – and that was rare enough over the past few months. But it wasn't just that. My anxiety, hopelessness and despair had all left me. I really did feel like a new man. Usually I stayed in bed for hours after I woke up, unable to face another pointless day. Today I felt full of energy. I couldn't wait to get up and get started.

After breakfast I went into Halifax. One of the things the Pastor had asked me to do was tell someone about my decision to follow Christ. Mum and Annette already knew, so I set off to find someone else. As I approached North Bridge – the place where only yesterday I had considered ending my life – I saw a man coming towards me. I didn't know him, but I caught his eye and smiled and said, "Do you mind if I tell you something?"

He stopped. "No, son, what is it?"

"Yesterday I gave my life to Jesus."

He didn't know what to say to that, but he gave me a smile and went on his way.

I didn't care if he thought I was a nutter. I just felt great that I'd accomplished what the Pastor asked me to do.

That was a really good day. First of all, Annette dropped in with some worship tapes – songs and prayers I could play on Mum's cassette player. Then someone from the church came round with a gift – a Bible of my own. I couldn't put that Bible down – I read it and read it, like someone starving who's been given some food.

I stopped going out at night – I didn't want to go to pubs and clubs any more. Instead I stayed home at Mum's, listening to those praise tapes with my Bible open in front of me, praying and praising God. Spending every evening in the presence of God was a lot better than the pub. Sometimes there was such a sense of awe in Mum's little front room, I felt as if God was there with me.

Of course, when I didn't turn up at the bookie's or the pub, people started wondering where I was. The phone rang – it was Jim.

"Hey, Peter. Coming out?"

"No, I'm stopping at home."

"Why, what's up?"

"I've become a Christian, Jim. I'm worshipping God."

Jim was dumbstruck. He turned up half an hour later. "What sort of gear have you got?" For him, it was the only explanation – I must be high.

"No, really, no drugs. It's God. He's changing my life."

"You're off your head, man." He walked out, disappointed that I had no drugs he could score off me.

In those early days it seemed that every time I opened my Bible I came across verses that spoke to me. In Acts 12:1–9 I read about another Peter, who was put in prison. God sent an angel to set him free. It sounded like a verse from an old hymn I'd heard at church:

> *Long my imprisoned spirit lay*
> *Fast bound in sin and nature's night.*
> *Thine eye diffused a quickening ray,*
> *I woke, my dungeon flamed with light.*
> *My chains fell off, my heart was free.*
> *I rose, went forth, and followed thee.*

In my case it didn't happen quite so fast. The light had come, and I had climbed up out of my dungeon step by step – but there were still a lot of issues for God to deal with. I had deep-seated habits, which had made me miserable and driven away the people (like Karen) I could have been close to. I'd spent years living in pain and misery, dwelling on thoughts of bitterness and revenge. I was addicted to drink, drugs and smoking. I had ways of seeking escape – like gambling and sex – which never worked, but that never stopped me trying. Over time, God was able to change all these patterns of behaviour and remake me as a new person. Right now I was still shackled to all these habits, and one by one, God struck off the chains that bound me to my past.

It was a miracle – just a miracle in slow motion.

Two of those chains were broken straight away: drinking and drugs. I never went back to either of them – the desire just left me. That in itself is amazing, given that I was physically addicted to both of them. For a long time I thought I was free of gambling, too – though I was to discover that chain was harder to break.

The next issue related to the time when I was stabbed. I had a very dark time after that, when I lost my job, my girlfriend and my independence. Even after I had physically recovered and got control of my life back, I went on dwelling on how I'd suffered and how I'd like to get my own back. I continued to have the fantasy about seeing the bloke who stabbed me – I knew I'd never forget his face – and beating him up. I thought that would make me feel better.

Once I started praying about it, God showed me how wrong I was. I couldn't get rid of my resentment through revenge. The only way to be free of those thoughts that kept coming back – the recurring nightmare of that snarl and the knife ripping into my arm – was to forgive.

I knew I couldn't go and find the man and make peace with him in person, so I did the next best thing. Just as, over the years, I had met him in my imagination to exact revenge, now I visualized meeting him again, only this time I replaced the beating with an explanation. In my mind, I went up to him in the pub and said, "You probably don't remember me. I'm the bloke you stabbed." He looked at me in fear, but I said, "It's all right, I'm a Christian. I forgive you." And I put my arm round him, gave him a hug and walked away.

That process did the trick. The thirst for revenge left me. The last of the wounds I received from the stabbing was finally healed.

I still had other resentment issues, like the matter of the hit-and-run accident. It was so unfair that the driver got away with it, while I was injured. God dealt with that one by reminding me of Jesus' bogus trial before Pilate. Jesus understands because he suffered injustice, and my injury was minor compared to his: the one holy and sinless Son of God, innocent of the trumped-up charges brought with no evidence, was taken from the court and killed. My not getting justice after the accident paled into insignificance.

The next chain to be removed was made up of cigarette-ends and ash-trays. For some reason I hadn't been able to give up smoking the way I'd given up drink and drugs. I was going to church, I was mixing with other Christians, and I was happy to count some of them as my friends. But none of them seemed to smoke and I knew that most of the time my clothes and hair reeked of tobacco. The Bible tells us that when God's Holy Spirit dwells in us, our body is his temple, yet I was pumping twenty fags a day into it.

It was so hard. I got my habit down to ten a day. Time after time I repented of it, I finished a packet full of determination, but within a few hours I'd find myself at the newsagent buying a pack of Benson & Hedges. I felt guilty.

I was lucky that God had put Jeff in my life – he was a good Christian friend and he knew how I felt about it. One day he said, "Peter, I've got to pray for you over this, OK?" He didn't mince his words:

"Father God, you know how hard Peter's finding it to give up. I pray that next time he lights up and takes a drag, it tastes like he's put his mouth over an exhaust pipe!" Well, at least it made me laugh.

The next day I lit up my first cigarette of the day, but it didn't taste right. I threw it away and opened a new pack. I lit another, and it tasted foul too. I put it out, and I haven't smoked a cigarette since. Another chain snapped.

There was another chain that took a while to break: sexual immorality. I hadn't been tempted in that way for a long time, but there came a day when I was struggling with my new faith, and I was feeling lonely and depressed. I was driving through a red-light district where prostitutes waited on street corners for passing business. I picked up a girl and we went back to her place.

Afterwards I apologized to the girl. "I don't know why I did that. I'm a Christian, I'm not supposed to give in to temptation. But I'm tired of being single and I was feeling low."

The girl said, "It's OK. I'm a Christian too. I know being on the game's wrong, but it's the only way I can get money. And I think God protects me when I'm out on the street."

I walked away from her house and thought, "I've really blown it. I've let God down. He won't want to know me now."

That evening I was sitting at home, sunk in gloom, when I heard a gentle voice speaking to my heart: "You need to repent." It was incredible – I thought my relationship with God was over, and yet he spoke to me. I got on my knees and cried, and asked for forgiveness. When I stood up, I felt clean again, and knew I was forgiven. The chain of immorality was broken, and I knew that God loved me, even though I had failed.

It's only when you're low and on the floor and God picks you up that you understand how much he loves you. I've let God down lots of times but he's always been faithful. And just as Jesus went out to be alongside the sinners and bring them the good news of God's love, so I believe he is with that prostitute, loving her and waiting for her to be ready to turn back to him.

There was one other issue that had to be sorted: my personal relationships. I was lonely and longed to have a girlfriend – perhaps even to get back with Karen – but I had a lot to learn, and God had plans for my life that I hadn't even dreamed of. Still, I knew that I had unfinished business with her and Peter Edward, and I wasn't in a position to ask anything of them. I went to see Karen and asked her to forgive me for the way I'd behaved. My whole lifestyle had been wrong, and I'd been selfishly trying to meet my own needs with drink, drugs and gambling, without thinking about her. We'd both been unfaithful in the past, but now I could see that wasn't any way to build a strong relationship.

"I don't want to get back together, Peter," she said.

"I'm not asking for that," I replied. "I just want you to know that I'm a Christian now and I'm learning to live in a different way. We need to be friends, at least, for Peter Edward's sake."

It was the best I could do.

I've told all these stories of how God freed me, bit by bit, from the chains of my past, because I think it's important for Christians to admit to their failures. It's too easy for Christians to tell the story of their conversion and make it sound as if God waved a magic wand and everything in their life was perfect afterwards.

When we give our lives to Jesus we are born again into new life, but becoming holy is a process which is never completed in this life. We are still human, and we still stumble and fall. But with the help of the Holy Spirit we can admit when we've failed, be forgiven, and grow stronger day by day as we walk with Jesus.

Chapter 6

Healing

About six months after I became a Christian, my mate Jeff – the one who prayed about my smoking – told me he knew of a room I could rent. Jeff went to an Elim Church and his pastor took in lodgers.

Moving in there was a blessing to me. Pastor Bob's house was in a Victorian terrace: the rooms were large and airy with high ceilings and big windows, and there was a garden. Best of all, there was a communal lounge for the use of the lodgers, so there was always company available if you wanted it. Sometimes we shared meals with the family – Bob, his wife Edith (who was a wonderfully compassionate and caring lady) and their two teenage sons. When I saw them saying grace together before eating, I thought it was wonderful. So this was what Christian family life was meant to be like. There was a sense of calm and security. It was so different from the chaos of my own childhood.

The house was regularly used for Bible study meetings by Bob's congregation, and although I was attending a different church in Bradford (the non-denominational Church on the Way), if I wasn't doing anything there, I'd join in. I always felt loved and accepted, even though I was so new to it all. I knew I was building firm foundations for my life as a Christian.

The other lodgers were a guy called John and a girl called

Jenny. I've no doubt that all three of us had emotional needs, and God had led us to this place of safety to renew and refresh us. One night I was in bed when I felt the Lord saying to me, "Go and knock on Jenny's door and see if she's all right." I hesitated for a bit, but in the end I got up and did it. When repeated knocking didn't rouse her I fetched Bob and we went in, to find that she had taken an overdose. Thankfully, we were in time. We rushed her into hospital and she recovered. That was when I found out that she had recently been divorced, and that like me, she struggled with depression. At Pastor Bob's we knew he and his family supported us, and we learned how to support and care for each other.

That summer I went to a Christian conference for the first time. What a mind-blowing experience that was! It was held at Holywell, in Cumbria, and consisted of a camp with tents and caravans round a conference hall. It was there I saw my first healings. There was a lady in a wheelchair who went up at a meeting to receive prayer, and she got up and walked. I was stunned – I'd read about things like that in the Bible, but I didn't know they still happened. When I was walking back to my caravan that night I passed her husband, pushing her empty wheelchair.

"That was wonderful," I said to him.

"Son, she hasn't walked for fifteen years," he answered. "It's amazing."

I felt really confused when I went to my prayers that night. So many people needed healing, but I knew that not everyone who asked was healed.

"I don't understand," I cried to God. Then I felt as if God

spoke to me:

"I don't want you to understand it," he said. "I want you to accept it."

I realized that having faith means trusting God, not understanding everything. Our human minds are limited, so we can't expect to fully understand God's ways.

One of the things I had learned from living at Pastor Bob's was how living as part of a Christian family could build your trust in God. I often thought how wonderful it would be to meet a Christian girl and have a family like his. So when I met Claire at that same conference, and found that she came from Halifax, like me, I was keen to get to know her better. I'd never been out with a Christian girl.

We started going to some of the meetings together, and chatting over coffee in between. She was lively and interesting and had a great faith. I really liked her and I felt we were becoming friends. In the past, as soon as a girl showed any interest in me, my first aim had always been to get her into bed. Now I found I had a different attitude of mind. Our evenings were spent praying and reading the Bible together, instead of focusing on drink, drugs and sex. I walked her back to her caravan at night without even thinking about making a pass at her. What was going on?

I had Claire's number, so when I got back home to Halifax I decided to ring her. I told her there was something on my heart I wanted to chat about, and asked if we could meet. She agreed, and we arranged to meet in the park one Saturday afternoon. I got there early, and spent fifteen minutes walking up and down, kicking stones along the path. I was really nervous about asking her out. When she arrived we went and sat on a park bench.

"So what did you want to talk about?" she asked.

I took a deep breath. "I had a great time at the conference last week. Since I got back I've been thinking about you a lot. Would you go out with me?"

There was a pause, then she turned to face me. She was a pretty girl, but at that moment I could see the Spirit of God in her, and it made her look really beautiful.

"Peter, just now it's not a girl you need in your life. When the time is right God will bring the perfect girl to you, but it's not me. God is working in your life, and I would be a distraction. He wants to build a foundation in you, and I don't want to get in the way of that."

It was probably the best turn-down in the history of dating, so gentle and caring, and done with such grace and wisdom. I didn't have a chance to feel upset. We chatted for a bit longer, and then she left. As I watched her drive away I was amazed at my reaction. Instead of feeling broken, rejected and depressed, I felt uplifted, edified and blessed. I believed that Claire was right, and God did have plans for my life.

That summer Peter Edward was three, and the arrangement with Karen was that I saw him on Saturdays. I'd pick him up at about 9 a.m., and take him home again at about 6 that evening. In between we'd go to the park or one of those children's indoor adventure centres, or visit my Mum. Annette had a little boy called Luke who was about the same age, so they played together a lot.

There was a fair amount of tension between me and

Karen. She didn't seem to acknowledge that my lifestyle had changed, and to her I was still the old Peter she'd left. For a long while I'd nursed a secret hope that we might get together again, but now she had a new partner. It gave me a jolt when Peter Edward chatted about "going in Robert's car". I had to struggle with my feelings of jealousy – Karen seemed to have got her life together – but I was always on my best behaviour when I picked up Peter Edward.

One Saturday morning I was watching Karen settle him into his child-seat in the back of my car, when I noticed what looked like a bruise on his neck. I didn't say anything, though. I thought I'd have a proper look when we got to Mum's house. It might just be dirt.

My brother John was at Mum's when we got there. I took Peter Edward's coat off and said, "Look at this." I licked my thumb and tried to wipe the mark away, but nothing came off. Mum said, "That's a bruise."

"Someone must've grabbed him round the neck," said John, "strangled him, like."

I went cold. I took Peter Edward into the bedroom and sat him on my knee.

"How did you get this mark on your neck, son?" I asked him.

"Robert came into my bedroom and strangled me, Daddy," he said.

I felt as if I was going mad. My little boy! Shock, fear and anger ran though me. I took Peter Edward back into the lounge to play, and went into the hall to try to ring Karen. There was no answer.

I had to do something. Desperate, I put Peter Edward in the car and drove to the police station. Once there, I told the policeman on the desk that my son had been strangled by his mother's new partner. He looked at the bruise and said, "Yes, I can see. That's not good, is it?"

We waited for quite a while in the lobby, and then a lady in a grey suit came out. She introduced herself as a Child Psychologist, took us into a different room and asked me what had happened. When I'd finished telling her, she said, "Do you mind if I talk to Peter Edward on my own?"

I went and waited outside, and ten minutes later she reappeared, holding Peter Edward by the hand.

"Everything's OK, Mr Gladwin," she said. "It's paint."

My jaw dropped.

"It's face-paint," she went on. "He went somewhere with his mum and had his face painted as an Indian. Most of it washed off but this bit is ingrained in his skin. I can perfectly understand your concern – it does look rather like a bruise."

I picked Peter Edward up and hugged him.

"Oh, Peter, why didn't you tell me?" I said.

Looking back, I think I can understand what happened. He was only three, and there had been a lot of changes in his life. He was missing me, he was aware of the conflict between me and his mum, and now he was having to get used to having Robert around. When John said "someone's strangled him" it must have put the idea in his mind.

On the way home in the car I wrestled with my feelings. Partly I was relieved that Peter Edward was OK, but part of me was almost disappointed. I suppose I thought it would cause a rift between Karen and Robert. I felt pretty stupid, too. "What a palaver," was Mum's only comment, but I spent the rest of the day wondering whether to tell Karen what I'd done. In the end I decided I'd have to. There was no way Peter Edward would keep quiet about his exciting trip to the police station.

When I took him home, I handed him over to his mum and explained. Karen was furious.

"You did *what*?" she shouted.

"I tried to ring you, but you weren't in…"

"That's it!" she said. "You'll never see Peter Edward again!" She shut the door in my face.

I was devastated. The old me would have banged on the door and shouted, but I didn't want to frighten Peter. I got back into the car feeling as though my world had collapsed in on me, and drove home hardly able to see the road for tears. I was crying out to God, "What's happening? Where's your plan in this?" but I couldn't hear an answer.

I tried to ring Karen several times that week, but she wouldn't talk to me. The next Saturday I went to collect Peter Edward as usual, but no one was in. Eventually I got through to Karen's mum, and she told me that they had moved and she didn't know where they had gone. That didn't seem likely – probably she just didn't want to tell me.

That was how I lost all contact with my son – for the crime of caring about his safety. It was a horrible time. I was trying to grow as a Christian, and understand concepts like joy and forgiveness, and at the same time I felt this deep sadness and loss, and anger at what Karen had put me through.

It plunged me into another deep depression for several

months. I would sit in my room, unable to summon up the energy to do anything, and brooding over the way I was missing out on my little boy's childhood.

Once again Jeff, my Christian mentor and supporter, came to my rescue. He walked in one day and said, "Peter, look at yourself. You're thirty years old, you've got no ties, you have the living God in your life, and you're still depressed! Get over yourself, and get a life."

My first reaction was that I wanted to strangle him! But when I calmed down I realized that it was a challenge from God. What good was I if I collapsed at the first difficulty in my life? I did pull myself together and got back on track, and I never looked back.

All the same, I thought about Peter Edward all the time, wondering what he was doing at every stage – starting nursery or starting school. I wrote letters to Karen at her mum's address, apologizing for being so hasty to assume the worst, but I never got a reply.

I had one other contact: when Peter Edward was six, Annette found out where he was living. Karen's new partner had a business in Halifax, and his home number was with the shop details. I wondered whether it would be better to leave my little boy undisturbed, but at the same time I longed to know how he was. Nervously I dialled the number, wondering what I'd say if Robert answered, and knowing that if I got Karen she'd be furious.

I rang at about 4 p.m., and to my delight, Peter Edward answered the phone.

"Hello?" he said.

"Is that you, Peter?"

"Yes, who is it?"

I was overwhelmed. Even though I hadn't spoken to him since he was three, I recognized his voice.

"It's your Dad!" I said.

"Me Dad's at the shop, he's just gone out," he said.

Before I could answer, Karen came into the room and took the phone from him.

"Who's that?" she asked.

"It's Peter," I said. "I just want to know how he is."

"How did you get this number?" she snapped, and then slammed the phone down before I had a chance to answer. I was so upset.

I didn't try to telephone again. But one day when I was in Halifax I drove out to see where they were living. It was a big stone farmhouse with fields all around. I felt thankful that Peter Edward was growing up in such a nice place.

In the years since then, I've made more attempts at contact, especially since Peter Edward became an adult. Once I heard that he was working in a pub, and I travelled up from the south of England to see him, only to find that he'd left that job. The barman gave me his phone number, and we had an awkward telephone conversation. I tried to explain how much I wanted to know how he was, but he was abrupt.

"Why d'you want to know now after all these years? Robert brought me up."

I was distraught.

"I'm getting ready to go out," he went on. "Don't call me again."

I have had to accept the pain of losing Peter Edward as part of the fallout from the damage in that part of my life, but I have never stopped loving him and wondering about him. In fact, the latest development has come about through Facebook: I found his page, and as it has no privacy restrictions on it, I can look and see what he's doing. It was wonderful to see his photo – he looks a lot like I did at his age. We have even exchanged messages on Facebook – I told him I'd found him, and he replied that he didn't blame me, but just wanted to get on with his life. I told him there was no pressure, but the door was always open.

Then, one New Year's Eve, I got the best present ever. My phone rang just after midnight, and it was Peter Edward saying, "Dad – Happy New Year." I just thanked him, but when I put the phone down I was crying. It had been so long, and I had missed out on all his growing-up years. I seem to have spent half my life wondering how he is, and who he is. I hope and pray that one day we can build a relationship based not on the past, but on who we are in the present.

Back in 1991 that was all in the future. I was still a young Christian, unsure what plans God had for my life, intent on growing and learning about the loving heavenly Father who cares for us.

The next amazing development was that my Mum became a Christian, too. She knew that both Annette and I had given our lives to the Lord. She herself hadn't been well, and then she had a heart attack and was rushed into hospital. When I saw her in that hospital bed, wired up to all the machines, I prayed that she might be healed. I didn't realize how thorough a job God was planning to make of it!

Maybe the heart attack made her start thinking about matters of life and death. I don't know. But one afternoon Annette rang me from Mum's flat and told me that she had led Mum to the Lord, just as she had led me. I was overjoyed. Mum was still quite frail, and I was so happy that she had learned to put her trust in God.

Then one evening Annette rang to invite me to an evening service at a church in Haworth — she and Mum were both planning to go.

When we got there the church was full of people who had come to hear the visiting speaker. It was a good service, with lots of lively hymns, and it was wonderful to be there with my Mum and my sister, praising God together.

Then the minister invited people to go forward for prayer, and Mum got up and made her way to the front, where a whole row of people were standing. I saw the minister stand in front of Mum, praying with her, when suddenly she fell backwards as though someone had knocked her over. Evidently the minister had expected this, because there was a man standing behind her to catch her, and he laid her gently on the ground. I had read about people being "slain by the Spirit" — apparently losing consciousness as God's power worked in them — but I'd never seen it before. I wasn't worried about her until I noticed that the minister had moved on to pray with the young man who was standing beside Mum — and there was no one behind to catch him. He could fall on Mum.

I jumped up and started making my way forward, but I was

too late. The young man fell backwards, and his outstretched arm struck Mum in the chest. Then he rolled off her. As soon as I got close enough to look at Mum, I knew something was wrong. She was deathly pale, and her eyes were rolling up into her head. Suddenly she started convulsing, her body rigid and shaking, and saliva frothing at the corners of her mouth.

I shouted for help, and a circle of people gathered around us. Annette had followed me, and we kneeled beside our Mum, terrified at what could be happening to her. A lady pushed through the crowd and said, "I'm a nurse, let me look at her." Then she turned to me and said, "Get an ambulance."

I rushed out of the church, pushing the chairs aside as I went. This was in the days before mobile phones, and I couldn't see a telephone box, so I banged on the door of the nearest house. When a man came to the door, I blurted out, "Can you call an ambulance for me? My Mum's in the church over there and she's having a heart attack."

When I got back to the church, Mum was lying in the recovery position. When the paramedics arrived, I think they were a bit bemused by all the people standing around praying. They put Mum on a stretcher and covered her with a blanket, and carried her out to the ambulance. Annette went with her to the hospital.

The nurse watched them leave and then turned to me and said, "I've seen a miracle tonight. Your Mum died shortly after you left. I checked her: there was no pulse, and she wasn't breathing. Everyone was praying, and a few minutes later, her pulse just started again. God brought her back from the dead."

I went back to Mum's place, wondering what was going on. I knew Annette would ring me there as soon as she knew anything.

At about eleven o'clock the door opened and Annette came in – followed by Mum, walking, talking, and generally OK. I couldn't believe my eyes.

"Mum! What are you doing here? What happened?"

"I'm all right," she said, "but I'm a bit tired. I'm just going to bed."

When she'd gone I turned to Annette. "What's going on?"

"I don't know. You saw how bad she was in the church. But they did loads of tests at the hospital and said she's fine, so they discharged her."

It seemed a bit odd, but we were just relieved that all the worry was over for the night.

A few days later I went to collect Mum's prescription as usual, but the pharmacist said there was something wrong with it, and I had to take it back to the GP. So I went back to the surgery and saw her doctor. He looked up Mum's notes and made the correction, but he seemed preoccupied.

"There's something here I don't understand."

"What do you mean?" I said. "I just need the prescription back."

"It's not that," he said. "We know your mum had a heart attack. Here are the X-rays – that white mark is the scarring that shows it was a serious attack. But she was taken to hospital a few days ago with another attack. I have the new X-rays here. The scarring has disappeared. Her heart looks healthy. In all my years of experience I've never seen anything like it. I don't understand it."

"I do," I said. I hadn't planned to say anything – it just came out. "Mum and me are both Christians. I believe God has healed her."

I hurried back to Mum's flat, ran in and hugged her.

"Mum," I said, "You're OK! God's healed you."

"Oh, put me down, son," she said.

When we told Annette, she didn't have any trouble believing it. "That's it," she said. "God's healed Mum's heart."

We went back to church the next week and told everybody about the miracle that had happened. It was such a boost to our faith to see God showing his love for us like that, and revealing his power in a miracle.

The problem is that when you start talking about miracles, people are dubious. They want proof. So a while later I went back to Mum's GP and asked him to put in writing what he'd said to me about Mum's healing, so I could read it out in church when I gave my testimony.

To my disappointment, he shook his head. "I can't do that, Peter," he said. "I believe in God myself, but I can't start putting my name to stories about miraculous unexplained healings. I'd be strung up by the Medical Council. I'm bound by their guidelines. I can't put anything in writing."

I understood, and though I was sorry not to have his affirmation of the healing, we didn't really need it – Mum is a very good advert for God's power. She has no major heart problems now other than mild angina. She gets about and does everything she used to do. She isn't one to talk about it very much, but she lives her faith quietly, caring for her family and praising God in her own way.

Chapter 7

A new life

The miracle of Mum's healing made my new faith even more exciting. I was keen to build on my relationship with God, and eager to learn more about what it really meant to be a Christian. I was hungry for the word of God, so I read my Bible every day, and went to church every Sunday, and to mid-week Bible studies as well. It seemed as if every day brought me new riches of understanding and joy.

There was another bonus which I hadn't expected. I was ready to have fellowship with God, but I hadn't known about the fellowship that exists between Christians. In the past I'd always been lonely: for years now I'd only mixed with criminals, drug dealers and users, people who had their own agendas. I'd been used and abused, sworn at, spat at, stabbed and robbed. My body bore the scars of a turbulent life, and these days I didn't expect ordinary people to give me the time of day. Yet now I was meeting people from all walks of life – not just factory workers and labourers but doctors and solicitors – and they accepted me without judgment or preconditions. It was as if the one thing we had in common – our love of Jesus – was more important than any differences in the rest of our lives. For me it was a transforming experience, and I was overwhelmed by the love of these people, and by the fact that I was valued by them. They showed me that I could be valued by God.

Curiously, one of the first results of this was that I got back into work. I had lost jobs previously through depression, and because of my addiction to drink and drugs. Now I was clean I started up my own little one-man business as a carpet cleaner. My mate Jeff lent me the money to buy an industrial-quality machine, and I put up adverts round the town. I didn't make a fortune, but it was enough to survive on and to repay Jeff quite quickly.

Meanwhile I was going on with my daily walk with Jesus, and all sorts of new ideas were dawning on me. At church I met several people who had been to Bible College. Imagine that – a college just for studying the Bible, and learning how to grow as a Christian. I'd never dreamed there could be such a thing. Of course, it would be ridiculous for me, a bloke who left school with no exams at all, to even think about it. But somehow the idea wouldn't go away. I wanted to go deeper with the Lord, to establish a sound foundation on which to build my life as a Christian, to enlarge my vision of what the Christian life could be. And above all, I wanted to grow closer to God. Surely, if these things could be learned anywhere, Bible College would be the place.

I talked about it to John, one of the other lodgers at Pastor Bob's. He didn't laugh at me. Instead he said, "Pray about it. If this idea's coming from God, he'll open the doors for you. Why not talk to Bob about it?"

Pastor Bob was a busy man, and it was hard to find a good moment for a chat, but the next day I went into the kitchen as he was making a sandwich for his lunch. I cleared my throat nervously, and he looked up.

"Hi, Peter. Did you want something?"

"I just wanted to ask you… I've been thinking… um… about going to Bible College. What do you think?"

Bob went on making his sandwich for a moment or two. I was so sure he'd start asking me what qualifications I had, or why I wanted to do it. Instead he just said, "That's a good idea. But how will you finance it?"

I was taken aback that he jumped straight to the practicalities. "Well, I suppose I'll have to apply to the Education Department for a grant."

"Sorry, Peter, you've got no chance. They don't give grants for that sort of course."

It was a funny thing, but now that Bob was saying no, I felt more sure that I could do it. Perhaps it was because he hadn't thought it was my ability that would be the stumbling-block, just the money. That was a problem that could be overcome. "Well, I've got to try. If God wants me to do it, the money'll come."

"OK," said Bob. "You get the forms, and we'll help you fill them in."

I sent away for the prospectus, posted my application, and waited. In due course I was invited to go for an interview, so I dressed up smartly and drove over to Nantwich. I nearly lost my nerve when I was parking the car. The college itself was an imposing building set in acres of beautifully landscaped grounds. It was the summer term, and there were little knots of students walking around with books under their arms, or sitting chatting on the grass. It was like something out of a film, and I felt uncomfortable. Did I really belong in a place like this?

I was interviewed by a panel of three academics. They asked me about how I became a Christian, about my life before my conversion, why I wanted to come to college, and what courses I would like to study. I answered everything honestly – I had nothing to hide. I told them that I felt I would struggle with the educational side of things, but I had overcome many difficulties in my life, and I was determined to succeed. They suggested that the degree course was likely to be too demanding for me, but that I should consider the two-year Certificate in Theological Studies and Pastoral Care. The only real problem was their final question: how was I intending to finance my course? I still didn't know the answer to that.

Somehow or other I must have impressed them, because three weeks later I received a letter offering me a place, "subject to finance". I had to get the money sorted out.

Having come so far, though, I refused to believe that I was going to fail now. Filling in the application forms for finance was a challenge in itself, but I managed it and sent them off. I knew it would be a while before I got an answer, but I stepped out in faith. I enrolled in the local further education college for a "Re-start" course in English. At school I'd been so busy bunking off and getting into trouble that I never mastered the basics; now I got to grips with punctuation, grammar, spelling and how to write an essay. It was tough but I stuck at it. To begin with I could hardly put a sentence together, but I knew that if I managed to get to college I'd have to write essays. I had to learn fast.

Then one day a brown envelope dropped though the door. I knew what it was, because it was franked by the local authority. I took it to my room, opened it and read the first words: "Dear

Mr Gladwin, you have been awarded a full financial grant to attend the Elim Bible College…"

Wow! I jumped off the bed, praising God, full of the joy of the Holy Spirit. People said it couldn't happen, but God made it happen – for me!

At tea time that afternoon all the family were gathered round the kitchen table. I handed my letter across to Pastor Bob, and watched his face as he read it. He smiled broadly, looked up at me and raised one finger in the air. "This is of the Lord," he said simply. It gave me goose-bumps. Once again I realized that not only had God forgiven and accepted me, but also he valued me and had a plan for my life. There, round that ordinary table, my Christian family prayed for me and committed my future to the Lord. I was on my way.

In September 1993 I packed my belongings in my car, ready to set off for college. Everyone in the house was standing on the drive, giving me hugs, wishing me well. Bob and Edith were there, for all the world like two parents seeing their son off to college for the first time. It felt wonderful – not only did I have this secure, loving group of friends behind me, but I was starting a new chapter of my life.

Of course, as soon as I was halfway down the road, the nerves set in. I had no idea what I was getting into, and the voice of insecurity in my head started up: "You're crazy, Peter. You can't do this. You were rubbish at school. You're only pretending to be a student. They'll soon find you out." I drove automatically, struggling internally between faith and fear, hurrying to reach my destination but wanting to put off my arrival for as long as possible.

Eventually I arrived and settled into my new room. There were three accommodation areas, and I was in Gilpin Block, named after Wesley Gilpin, one of the heroes of the Elim movement. I set up the new computer I had bought out of my savings, and the reference books I'd been told to get. Then I went out to meet my fellow students.

That first weekend was amazing. Everyone was full of excitement and anticipation, and everyone had a different testimony of how the Lord had provided for them to get there. Many of the other students had come from abroad, and coming to England was a dream come true for them. I had never been outside England, but now I was making friends from all over the world.

The only fly in the ointment was Andrew, a student from Ireland. He was a gifted musician and singer, and very confident in his own abilities (later I discovered he never got less than 80 per cent in any of our exams). As soon as I opened my mouth he must have realized I was someone with hardly any education. He looked at me in amazement and said, "What are you doing here?" I was shocked. I thought, "Surely he knows I've been called here by the Lord!" but I wasn't brave enough to say anything. To be honest, if he'd spoken to me like that before I became a Christian, I'd have punched his lights out. Now I just bent my head and kept quiet.

Andrew's attitude knocked me back badly. Alone in my room that night, all my doubts came flooding back, and when I walked into the classroom for the first time on Monday morning I was shaking with a mixture of fear and pride. I'd got there. But could I manage the work? I was even more scared when we were given our first assignment: a 2,000-word essay on the attributes of Jesus, complete with footnotes giving our sources and a full bibliography.

I worked furiously all week, consulting all my books, writing notes, and typing them up with one hand (because I have no fingers on my left hand). I was thrilled when I finished it in good time, the day before the deadline. Success! I could do this!

I pressed one final button to save it, and then tried to print it. Nothing. I was still learning my way round the computer, so I went and got a friend to help me, and he looked in all my files. No sign of it. Somehow I'd managed to delete my essay.

I stormed out of the accommodation block into the chilly night air, and walked around in a fury. "I told you I couldn't do this!" I said to God. "You wouldn't believe me! Why did I fool myself into thinking I could manage it? I'm too stupid to work a computer."

I found a bench among the flowerbeds and sat down. When I finally ran out of things to call myself, I cried. That was when I heard the voice of God speaking in my heart. He was gentle but firm: "Don't be discouraged or dismayed. My favour is upon you. Now get back in there. You've got a lot of work to do."

I groaned, but I was comforted. Anyone could make a mistake with unfamiliar technology. I'd written that essay once, so I could do it again. It just meant time and effort, and I could put both of those to the task. I went back to my room, got out my notes, opened my books, and got started. It was going to be a long night.

I was shattered the next day when I handed my paper in, on time. A week later I got the marked essay back: I'd scored 60 per cent. I was delighted – the pass mark was 53 per cent. I reminded myself that trust in God is always repaid, provided you're willing to do what he says.

In my second week I had another reminder of God's ways. One of my new friends was George, who came from Ghana. God told me, "Give George £500."

"What?"

I didn't have much more than that in the bank, and it was money I'd been saving to support myself during the course. I battled with myself, but I knew I had to take up God's challenge. George had never said anything about needing money, though now I came to think of it, he had been looking a bit worried lately. I wrote a cheque and went and found him. When he looked at it his mouth dropped open.

"What's this?"

I told him.

Tears filled his eyes. He had been praying for that money: he needed £500 as the final payment for his fees, and without it he would have had to abandon the course and go home. I had made a friend for life – and somehow, even without my savings, I always seemed to have just enough money for my own needs while I was at college.

The rest of the year flew by. I was learning how to study, writing essays and managing not to delete them, meeting new people, socializing, developing friendships, and growing in faith and confidence. As well as academic work, we all had to undertake service in a local church. I was placed in a church in Sandbach with some fellow students, and we did anything we were asked, whether that was leading a service or making the tea. It was a good way to learn about servanthood and humility: some of the "ordinary Christians" in that church knew a lot more about their faith than we did. I learned how to work in a church fellowship, how to give unconditionally of my time and energy and be part of a fellowship. I was happy.

Then, suddenly, it was exam season. I revised hard, but I'd never taken an exam like this before, and something happened to me when I got into that exam room. The silence got to me. Everyone else was bent over their papers, scribbling furiously, and I just fell apart. I stood up and went up to the invigilator sitting at the front of the room.

"Do you mind if I leave? I can't go on."

I went outside and stood in the yard, feeling like an emotional wreck. At the end of the exam everyone else came out, chattering excitedly, relieved that the first ordeal was over. I didn't want to talk to anyone.

Fortunately the lecturer in charge had informed the college Principal, John Smith, about my walking out, and he called me into his office.

"Peter, what happened to you in there? I've been looking at your course work, and all your marks are good. Considering your educational history, your progress has been amazing. There's no reason why you shouldn't be able to do that exam."

I couldn't explain it – it was as though the whole atmosphere of the exam room overcame me. I never found it easy to get my thoughts down in writing, though I was fluent enough when I spoke about what I had learned. Perhaps I just wasn't cut out for academic work.

Dr Smith looked thoughtful.

"You know, being a Christian isn't about academic theology. Neither is this course: it's about balance. As long as you can understand the Bible and its themes, and combine that with your passion for the Lord and for sharing your faith, you'll succeed. I have a suggestion. In future, you can take all your exams orally. That means when the others go into an exam, you come to my office. I will ask you the same questions, and you can tell me your answers. Do you think that will work?"

I thought it would.

Dr Smith was an amazing man – scholarly but humane, with great compassion and wisdom. He understood where I had come from, and what a struggle I'd had to get as far as this. His words lifted me up from the depths of despair, and inspired me with hope. I took all my remaining exams in the way he described, and I passed every one of them.

That summer vacation we were asked to choose a project, and I chose to join a missionary organization called Operation Mobilisation, which seeks to demonstrate and proclaim the love of God in every region of the world (and on every ocean, via its ocean-going ship, the *Logos*). OM was running a conference in Holland, and some of us travelled to attend it, and to be interviewed and placed in missionary teams. My team then moved on to run a mission in Tidderholm in Sweden, about two hours' drive from Stockholm.

I don't know what I had expected, but I was pleasantly

surprised when I saw where we would be staying for the next two weeks. A basement had been converted to provide good accommodation: brand new sofa-beds, a kitchen, a fridge, and a larder full of food. The people of that church really spoiled us.

We were asked to take part in street evangelism, standing up in parks and shopping centres with a worship team, speaking about our faith through an interpreter. We met lots of young people (some of them skinhead gangs), we did drama and question-and-answer sessions, and we were amazed at how well our efforts were received. The host church was encouraged by our visit, and we were encouraged by the number of people who made a commitment to Christ, and started coming along to the church as a result. It was a fantastic couple of weeks – it felt like a holiday to me, seeing new places and meeting new people. Talking about the Lord I loved and trusted certainly didn't feel like work.

After the mission we returned to the OM centre in Holland for a "debrief" session. While I was there reporting back on my experiences, I met up with a girl who had been on a different team. Before the mission she had been bubbly and excited, but now she looked tired and dejected. She asked me how my mission had gone.

"Fantastic, thanks," I said. "They treated us really well, and we felt we made a difference in their town. What about yours?"

"It was depressing, to be honest," she replied. "We went to Latvia, and there were five of us in one room, sharing two beds. It was dirty and we didn't get enough to eat. There were rats running over us at night, so I didn't get much sleep. I've never seen such poverty. It was hard to believe that we could achieve anything in the face of that deprivation."

My heart went out to her. She had been at the sharp end of mission, really struggling to make a difference for God, while I'd been snugly in my comfort zone, well housed and looked after and engaged in well-organized activities. Later on, though, I wondered whether perhaps God in his wisdom was dealing with each of us according to our needs. That girl had probably never encountered deprivation, never experienced overcrowding before. Her eyes were opened and she was now on her way to a new maturity. Although I felt somewhat guilty for having been given a relatively easy ride, my greatest need was for affirmation and confidence-building, and by God's grace I had received it.

There was one last event in that summer that I'll always remember. We returned to England on the overnight ferry, and early the next morning I was lying in my bunk when I felt God saying, "Go up on the deck." I didn't really want to – I was enjoying lazing in my cabin – but when someone tapped on my door and said, "Coming on deck, Peter?" I knew I had to go. When I got there I found thirty or so of the students who had been on mission trips, all sharing with the other passengers about what they had been doing. There was no way you could explain about going on a mission without your passion and fire for the Lord's work being clear to everyone. After my experiences in Sweden I found I had a new boldness, enabling me to stand up and address a crowd, telling people what I'd been doing and why. It was at that moment that I began to realize that perhaps God was planning to use me in evangelism. It's great to receive salvation, but God has a work for us to do. It's not just about saving ourselves – we are participants in his mission to save the world, and I wanted to be an evangelist and tell people about the good news.

I went back to Elim Bible College for my second year full of optimism. I had mastered new study skills, overcome my lack of confidence and got to grips with the mysteries of my computer. I never missed an essay deadline and I always got my project work in on time. Sometimes I looked a little enviously at the students to whom it all came easily: one guy would flick through his books for a couple of hours and get 90 per cent, while I spent a week revising and managed to achieve a little above the pass mark. I never got really high marks, but I plodded stolidly onwards, because I knew what I was aiming at.

In the spring break a group of us went to Spain with the Elim church. This was a particularly strenuous mission: for a start, we drove there, camping en route. At least when we arrived in Alicante the weather was good (our tent had been flooded in heavy rain on our way through Belgium). It was a fruitful mission, too, and we saw people giving their lives to Christ and being introduced into local church fellowships. It was very encouraging. Back at home I joined more mission events in Nantwich and Crewe, and by then I was feeling much more confident about what I was doing. The only problem as far as I was concerned was that one of the people in my team was Andrew, the brilliant student who had put me down so hard on my first day at college. I still felt intimidated – everything came so easily to him. Having him around made me nervous, so I prepared extra carefully whenever it was my turn to preach. It seemed to go down well, but afterwards I realized that whatever I had done or said, it was from the wrong motives. I just wanted to prove to Andrew what a good evangelist I was. I knelt before God and prayed:

"Lord, what have I done? It's not about me, it's about you. That's where my focus should be – on doing your will, not impressing other people."

I went over to Andrew's room that evening and said, "Let's talk." I told him how I'd been feeling, and explained that I'd never forgotten what he had said to me that day, and how much it had hurt me. Andrew was horrified.

"What I said was totally out of order," he confessed. "I should never have made those assumptions about you, and I shouldn't have opened my mouth and spoken them." He begged my forgiveness, and I felt that we had turned a corner. I wouldn't let it worry me any more.

When I got back to college there were still a few days before the start of the summer term, so most of the students hadn't come back yet. The only people in college were our group returning from missions, and a handful of new students about to start short courses. One of these was a stunning blonde called Sarah. She caught my eye as soon as I walked into the common room, and I managed to get into conversation with her. I soon discovered that her beauty wasn't just external: she glowed with gentleness, kindness and her love of Jesus. I also found out that she was Swiss, just arrived for a short English course, and only nineteen (I was thirty-two). I decided that I had no chance with her; besides, in a couple of days all the rest of the students would arrive, and all the handsome young stallions would be competing for her attention. A scarred and disabled mature student wouldn't have a hope.

A couple of weeks passed, and it was clear that no one else had dared make a move either, so I invited her to see a film. It was a casual arrangement – there were four of us – but after that we spent a lot of time together, often sitting up chatting till 2 a.m. Eventually I plucked up the courage to ask her if she'd come out on a date with me. She hesitated. "Peter, I feel we should just be friends," she said.

Of course, I could only agree, but I couldn't get her out of my mind. I prayed about her, asking God to help me give up and move on, but his voice spoke in my heart: "She doesn't mean it." That was hard to believe – surely it was just wishful thinking on my part.

"OK, Lord, I hand it all over to you. If it's your will, please bring her back to me."

I felt that my prayer needed something more – something to prove to God how serious I was about this lovely girl. I decided to go on a three-day fast. If nothing had happened after that, I would accept that it wasn't God's will that we should be together, and that I had lost her.

Six hours later I was walking across the garden when I saw Sarah sitting on a bench. She looked sad.

"Sarah, are you OK?"

"No, not really."

"Why? What's wrong?"

"Can we talk?"

"What about?"

"You and me. We need to pray."

That was one rapid response to prayer: six hours into my fast (I'd barely missed a meal) and God had answered me. We agreed to pray about our relationship, and handed the issue over to God together, asking him for his guidance. We both knew that we were getting into something serious.

The next thing that happened was that I went on a mission in Wales, and while there a lovely Christian lady told me, "I believe I have a message for you from the Lord. He is bringing a girl into your life." I was overjoyed, and told her all about Sarah and me. It was yet another confirmation that God cares about our lives, and speaks to the people who are listening to him. I couldn't wait to get back to college and tell Sarah.

"You'll never guess what! God's spoken to me about our relationship..." I stopped. Sarah wasn't looking hopeful. "What's happened?"

"I rang my mum and told her about you. She's worried. She says she'll pray about it."

Sarah's dad had died when she was six, and Erika, her mum, had brought up their three daughters alone. I knew that she was a Christian, but even so, I was concerned. Would she hear the same message as my friend in Wales? Or would she be influenced by her concern for her daughter? I had been honest with Sarah about my past life – the crime, the drink, drugs and gambling – and of course I bore the scars of all those accidents and attacks. If she had told her mum everything, no wonder she was worried.

I need not have been concerned, because God's hand was

on us. That week a German evangelical magazine dropped through Erika's letterbox. It contained an article about an English guy whom God had taken from a life of chaos and crime and placed in Bible College. There was a picture, taken the previous summer, with the caption, "Peter Gladwin witnessing to a crowd of fascist skinheads in Sweden."

Erika had been planning to come to England for Sarah's birthday, so she brought the magazine with her. When she got to the college she showed Sarah the article. "Is this the man you were telling me about?"

Sarah nearly fainted when she saw the picture. "Lord, I don't need any more confirmation," she said. Two months later we got engaged.

Even our engagement was marked by Christian fellowship and love. A week before Sarah's course ended and she flew home to Switzerland, we were having a meal in the home of some friends in the Sandbach church where I was placed. There was another couple there called Steve and Jane, and they were interested in our story of how we had been brought together. Of course, I didn't have any money to buy an engagement ring, but I told them that as soon as I got a job I would buy one and post it to her.

"That doesn't sound very romantic," said Steve. We had never met before, but at the end of the meal he called me over and gave me a cheque for £100. "The Lord has told me to give you this. Go out tomorrow and get that ring, and send your fiancée home with it on her finger!"

I was sad when Sarah had gone home – partly because I missed her, but also because it was the end of my course and of a wonderful chapter in my life. Three days before the end of term a graduation ceremony was held in the hall. I wasn't planning to attend, because my own awards ceremony (for the people getting diplomas and certificates) was later in the week, but at the last minute I decided to go along. I clapped as people received their degrees, and then I heard the Principal say, "The award for the most improved student at Elim Bible College, 1995, goes to Peter Gladwin."

I was stunned. I had won an award for studying! Three hundred students stood up and cheered and threw their mortar-boards in the air – for me! It was a beautiful moment. I got to the rostrum with tears running down my face. Dr Smith said, "It's an honour to give you this award. You've worked so hard, and it's been a privilege to meet you."

I gulped back my tears and stepped up to the microphone. I raised my award in one hand and said, "I'd just like to say this. We'll all be leaving this college in three days' time. Just remember, the Bible says, 'Nothing is impossible for God', and I've just proved it!"

Two days later Mum and Annette drove up for the final awards ceremony, and saw me receive my Certificate in Theological Studies and Pastoral Care. Then they went home, and I spent another couple of days packing up my things and saying goodbye to friends. I was driving to the gate for the last time when I saw Andrew standing on the grass. As I drove towards him he pointed one finger up to the sky, and then started clapping. My last sight in the college was of him applauding me as I drove out of the gate.

I wept and praised God as I drove home, thanking him for his faithfulness. "Lord, I could never have done all this, but only in your strength." The future, I felt, was full of good things.

Chapter 8

Seeking guidance

Shortly before I left Bible College I had a strange encounter. My friend Sheila from the Sandbach church showed me a newspaper cutting about a young man called Paul who had been involved in an accident. The car he was travelling in had left the road and hit a tree; his friends were killed instantly but Paul was trapped in the burning car until a passer-by heroically dragged him out. He suffered extensive burns to his whole body. Now, six months after his release from hospital, he was deeply depressed, and the article asked what help there was for someone who had suffered like this.

"You're always positive about your injuries," Sheila said to me. "Couldn't you go and see him?"

I didn't see how I could help – I wasn't a counsellor – but I didn't feel I could refuse, so I made contact and drove up one Sunday to see him. Paul was a big chap, about six feet tall and broad with it, with blond hair. His face hadn't been burned at all, so he looked absolutely normal. His parents left us together, and I wondered what to say. I asked him about his accident, and he told me about it very briefly – he didn't seem to want to go into the details.

Then I told him that I'd been in a fire as a baby. I took off my shoes and showed him the stumps of my feet, and the scars on my legs, arms, face and neck. That seemed to unlock something and he said, "Would you like to see what happened to me?" I got the feeling he'd been afraid to show anyone, in case they were repulsed by the sight of him. He took off his shirt, and I saw that his injuries were horrific. His skin wasn't yet completely healed, and it was a violent red, like raw steak. The burns covered his torso and legs as far down as his ankles, front and back. I looked without flinching.

"Boy, that's pretty, isn't it?" I said.

Paul started talking about how he felt. His girlfriend had left him and now he thought he'd never get another girl. He was in a daze about what the future held.

I just listened. I didn't try to minimize what he was going through, or try to cheer him up by saying that I was OK and that he'd get over it. I agreed that the next few years were going to be a challenge, and told him that I'd had to dig deep to accept my disability and not let it beat me. I just tried to do my best at everything. Then I told him how low I had fallen, and how I'd found Jesus at the crucial moment to save my life.

We spent the day together, and after dinner Paul said, "There's a little church in the village. Shall we go?" We went to church together that night. When the Pastor asked if anyone would like to go forward for prayer, Paul got up and went, without any prompting from me. When I left him that night he put his arms round me and thanked me for coming.

I don't know what I did to help Paul, but I know he did something for me. Up until then I had never seen anything positive about all the terrible things that had happened in my life. I'd never whinged about my condition, but I'd always seen it as a handicap which prevented me from doing what I wanted. Now I saw that perhaps good could come out of it. I felt as though I'd been released from something that had always weighed me down, as if my terrible history could be redeemed by God into something beautiful – giving people comfort. Even then I didn't see it as something vocational, but it planted the seed of a thought: perhaps my experiences had the potential to help other victims of injury and suffering.

I left Bible College on a high. It had been such a wonderful time, being surrounded by other Christians who prayed for me and encouraged me. I began to believe that God had plans for my life. Sarah was back in Switzerland, but I knew that before long we would be together again. The future looked good.

Although everyone at college had said I had the potential to be an evangelist, I had a secret desire to work in prisons. One of the first things I did was to go on a "taster" course for prison chaplaincy. I didn't feel that it was a great success. I spent a day in a prison, shadowing a Church of England chaplain, which I enjoyed – I felt that I could relate to prisoners better than some of the middle-class, university-educated ministers around me. I also attended a couple of seminars with other interested candidates, all of them already vicars. One of them asked me, "Where's your dog-collar?" I bit back the reply, "In my heart." I could see that I didn't really fit in. After the course I applied for a job but I never got a reply.

After that rejection, I decided that the obvious place to use my gifts was as a missionary. I had been inspired by my contact with Operation Mobilisation, especially their mission ship, the *Logos*. I began dreaming of trips to Brazil and Chile, spreading the word of the Lord. The church in Sandbach had agreed to sponsor me as a missionary candidate, and George Verwer himself, the founder of OM, had prayed over me when he visited the college. I was certain that this would be my path, so I went off immediately to another OM conference in the hope that this would open the right doors.

The conference was just like the others I'd attended, buzzing with the excitement of missionary teams going off around the world. However, there was one hint that all was not well. As I sat in the conference hall, listening to a presentation, I heard God speak in my heart: "Peter, what are you doing here?"

"Lord," I answered, amazed that he was asking, "I'm getting ready to go on a ship, to do your work."

The next day I had my interview with the *Logos* personnel department. I told them I had the backing of my church and the finance was all in place. Then they dropped the bombshell. They told me that they were rejecting my application: they didn't believe it was the right thing for me.

"What?" I thought. "Please God, no!"

The chairman told me why: they didn't believe I was physically strong enough for the rigours of life on board, and they thought my amputations would hinder me. I was amazed. It was true that I couldn't run a mile or walk for long distances, but I functioned all right in daily life. I was devastated by their decision.

"What we'd like you to pray about," the chairman went on, "is joining a field team working with drug addicts in southern Spain."

That made some sort of sense: after all, I had already

worked in Spain and I knew people there. It seemed like a sensible alternative, so I agreed.

"When would I be going?"

"Next Tuesday," was the answer. Well, that seemed a bit of a rush, but I supposed I could do it. Reluctantly but obediently I gave up my dream of sailing on the *Logos*. After all, the important thing was to be working for the Lord, not doing whatever I thought would be exciting. I returned to the main conference saddened but optimistic.

Back in the hall, I heard that voice again: "What are you doing here?"

I tried to shut it out, but I couldn't. "Lord, I'm getting ready to go to Spain for you."

Back came the answer I feared: "No, you're not. I want you to go home to England."

I tried to persuade myself that it was my own disappointment speaking, that I could ignore it and carry on, but I knew that wasn't the case. God was shutting the door to missionary work.

The next day I went back to the OM board and told them what had happened. They all agreed that I needed to return to England, so I set off with a heavy heart. I had left with such high hopes, and now I was going back with my tail between my legs, uncertain of anything.

I found lodgings with a couple in Cheshire, and got myself a job as an assistant carer, working nights in a home for the elderly – I wasn't qualified for anything else. In fact, I enjoyed it. I liked talking to the old people, and they appreciated a friendly smile from someone prepared to chat to them.

The only sad thing was that most of them were very frail and there were frequent deaths. It was a sobering lesson to me: life was such a fleeting thing. Over the years they had accumulated so much knowledge, experience and wisdom, and then death came and just snuffed it out. If you didn't believe that there was something more waiting beyond this life, it would be very depressing. Here were these people, all individuals precious to God, and they were so humble; they knew their deaths were imminent. It comforted me to think that they would go on into the next life. Sometimes when someone passed away there would be a strange, almost holy atmosphere in the room, as if you could feel an angelic presence.

One evening I went in to work as usual, and called in on an old lady called Doris. She was in her nineties, and ever since I'd known her she had been lying curled in a foetal position in her bed. She always had her eyes shut and she never spoke. She must have roused a bit during the day to eat and drink, but I never saw it. I always went in and greeted her cheerfully, just as if she was awake and aware of me, though I never got any response.

On this night I was tidying her room and chatting away, and on impulse I said, "Doris, do you know God loves you? Jesus died for you, and he's just waiting to accept you into his family. But of course, we've all got to say sorry to him – we've all let him down, you know." There was the usual silence, so I finished what I was doing, said goodnight, turned out her light and left.

The next night I went in and found her bed empty.

"Where's Doris?" I asked the supervisor.

"Peter, you wouldn't believe it," she said. "She woke up this morning bright as a button, chatting and singing. She asked to get out of bed, so we put her in a chair in the conservatory in the sun. Someone went in an hour later and she was dead."

It may sound odd to say that someone's death cheered me up, but this one did. I had no doubt that Doris was with the Lord, and that she had died in that knowledge.

In general, though, I was feeling pretty low. The only glimmer of light on the horizon was Sarah: I knew she would be returning to England and we would get married eventually, but we had no idea when. Meanwhile my job wasn't well paid, and I had an overwhelming sense that I'd been here before. I was disillusioned about my spiritual life, and questioning God's plan. I dealt with my black moods by working harder and harder: I was working the night shift in the care home, but I also took on some part-time care work during the day, visiting people at home. I would get a couple of hours' sleep in the morning and then get up and go out again. I was driven by my need to get money together for the wedding.

It took a long time. I reckoned we needed at least £3,000, and after six months or so I only had £1,000. I was absolutely exhausted by doing two jobs, and my old enemy, depression, was haunting me. One day, while I was in this low state, I passed a betting shop, and instead of walking on by, I gave it a second look. I could feel God's voice within me saying, "Don't go in there," but I was tempted. Stress and tiredness affects you in many ways. In my case, I lost my focus on trusting God, and old habits of thought took over. It was such a simple way of multiplying my money! A couple of successful bets would do it.

While the mood lasted, I was obsessed. I bet my money in fifties and hundreds, and as usual I would gain a bit, then lose a bit. All the time I could feel God saying, "Get out of here!", but the old excitement was stronger. In the end, I lost the lot – the whole £1,000. All that hard work for nothing. I didn't even have the money to pay my rent.

Worse followed. I went home and confessed to the couple I lived with that I'd gambled my money away, and they told me to leave. At the time I thought they were heartless – surely as Christians they should have treated me with more charity – but later I could see their point of view. They had a young family themselves, and they knew the background I'd come from. They had seen for some time that I wasn't right with myself or God – I was tired and depressed and irritable – and they thought I was backsliding and would end up bringing drink or drugs into their home. I packed my bags and got into the car, wondering what to do next.

In a way, my landlords were right. In the old days, I would have found solace in drink and drugs. But I wasn't in that dungeon any more. I might have slipped down a few steps in that betting shop, but that wasn't the way I wanted to live my life. I wasn't acting in my own strength, but in God's, and he works through his Holy Spirit in us and in others. Friends and fellowship were what I needed.

On impulse I drove to the coast and took the ferry to France, where I had a friend working as an evangelist. His parents were missionaries, and they welcomed me in and listened to my tale of woe. It was a humbling and healing week. They prayed for me and talked to me, and gradually I came to understand what had happened. There is always a battle going on in our spiritual lives, and there are forces at work trying to knock us off track and derail God's plans. If we're immature and ignore God's voice (and I had certainly heard and ignored it while I was in that betting shop), they tip us over. Fortunately, God is always there waiting to pick us up.

I still believed that God had a plan for my life. What was frustrating me was that I didn't know what it was. I kept trying to give him a helping hand that he didn't need: I tried to set myself up to work in prisons by arranging the chaplaincy course; I couldn't wait to find out how God wanted to use me as an evangelist, so I tried to hurry things along by deciding that I wanted to work for OM; I couldn't wait and work for the money I needed to get married, so I tried to win it by gambling. Whenever I tried to act in my own strength and according to my own timetable, I came to grief. What I needed to learn was how to trust God and wait on him.

They advised me to return to England, to find somewhere to live, to get back into a church fellowship that would support me and keep me grounded in my faith, and to seek God's will – without pushing him for easy answers. I drove home feeling considerably better. Going to France had been impulsive (and it had used up the very last of my cash) but it had been worth it.

I still had the problem of accommodation, however, but as I prayed about it I had a brainwave. A couple of months before my life had collapsed in on me, I had given a lift to a homeless lad on his way to Crewe. He asked me to take him to the YMCA hostel, and as he got out of the car, I thought, "I'd never live in a place like that." Now I drove back along the same route, and soon I found myself in the foyer of the same YMCA, telling them I was homeless and asking for a room.

Fortunately (and as I later discovered, in a departure from their usual practice) they let me in straight away. At least I would have somewhere to sleep that night. As I wearily climbed the stairs to my room, I knew that my pride was broken. Everything I owned was in a suitcase. I had the key to a tiny room, with a bed, a wardrobe, a table and a lamp. And yet I felt oddly at peace. I felt secure, because God was with me. I realized that all the theology I'd learned at Bible College wasn't enough: to cope with life you needed character. What was my Christian character like? Was it puffed up with its learning and diplomas, or was it humble and ready to listen to God's voice?

Even then, it took a while for me to accept my situation. I was in the communal kitchen one day when I met another resident, a rough-looking guy with the bloodshot eyes and shaky hands of a drinker.

"How long you bin here, lad?" he asked me.

"Oh, a couple of weeks. But I won't be here long. This is only temporary," I said. "I'm a Christian. God's told me he's going to get me a flat."

"Yeah? That's a good one. You'll be here for years, like me."

His words were like a dagger. I knew he could be right.

Still, I was determined to follow the advice I'd been given, and get my life back on track. The first thing I did was to find a church, and get back into a fellowship of prayer and praise. I made friends there, and they kept me from getting too depressed about being unemployed and having no money. It wasn't easy – my prospects for earning enough money to get married seemed worse than ever.

Then one night after a Bible study meeting, my mate Howard offered me a lift home. On the way, he said, "Do you mind if we make a detour to the station? I've promised to pick up a friend."

"No, of course, that's fine," I said, thinking it would probably have been quicker to walk home. Howard disappeared into the station, and I stood beside the car, deep in thought.

When I looked up, I noticed a girl walking towards me – a beautiful girl with long blonde hair just like Sarah's. I did a double take: it *was* Sarah!

"Peter!" she called, and ran up to me. My heart was pumping with excitement as I took her in my arms. I was so confused – why hadn't she told me she was coming?

Then Howard came back, and I realized it had all been a conspiracy between my friends at church. They could see how low I was, and they'd planned to bring Sarah over to cheer me up. I was stunned by their kindness.

The only problem was how to explain to Sarah where I'd ended up. I plucked up my courage. After all, I'd told her all about my past and she'd accepted me. I'd have to tell her about my present situation, and hope she could forgive me. While Howard drove, I told her all about my gambling, becoming homeless, and that I was now reduced to living in the YMCA. Of course, being Swiss, she didn't know what that meant.

"Is it nice?" she asked. "I can't wait to see it."

I had to get permission for Sarah to see my room, but when I explained that she was visiting a local church family and wouldn't be staying the night, she was allowed to come upstairs.

She looked around and said, "It's beautiful, Peter."

What? This poky room? Then I looked at it again through her eyes, and remembered how safe I'd felt that first night when I'd arrived. It was a beautiful room, because God had given it to me, and it was a safe haven while I picked myself up again. I had expected Sarah to be shocked at how low I'd fallen, but I'd forgotten how optimistic she always was. And I'd forgotten that, amazingly, she loved me.

We had a wonderful weekend together, and made plans for our future – we decided that the money wasn't important, but being together was. The church I attended met in a room above a public library, and wasn't licensed for marriages, so we had to find somewhere else for the wedding. We decided on St Mary's in Sandbach, a beautiful old Anglican church in the High Street. We fixed the date for 26 October 1996.

Sarah went back to Switzerland, telling me not to worry about anything, but to get a job and cut out the gambling. No one was ever so willing to do what his future wife demanded! I promised her that I'd make a new start, knowing that it was her love and forgiveness that gave me the courage and strength to work for our future together. It was a reflection of my relationship with God: how often do we have to make the same promise to him, and how often does he have to forgive us and go on loving us?

In this case, God showed me his faithfulness once again: I

found a flat in Sandbach, immediately across the road from the church where we planned to marry. It was only a bedsitter with a bathroom, but it was clean, light and airy, and big enough for both of us to start out in. The only problem was that I hadn't yet got a job, and I didn't have enough money for a deposit. I explained this to the owner, Stuart. His answer amazed me:

"Here are the keys. You can move in tonight, and I'll fix the rent to match your benefits. You can pay me when you get your Giro."

I've no idea why he was so helpful. He didn't know me, he didn't ask for references or for a deposit, and he took my word that I'd pay my rent. I can only conclude that it was God's doing.

I went back and packed my suitcase at once. I was so thankful to the YMCA for giving me a home when I needed one, and I prayed for all the people I was leaving behind. I called in on the bloke I'd met in the kitchen and told him I was leaving, but I wasn't gloating. I just wanted him to know that our God is a faithful God who delivers on his promises. Right now I don't suppose for a moment that every bit of my pride has been finally dealt with, but the Peter who left the hostel that day was a different man from the one who had felt so crushed by his circumstances on his arrival. I had learned a new humility. Now I was determined to walk more humbly with Jesus; I felt that I had been granted another new beginning.

Once I was settled in the flat, everything seemed to go better. Almost at once I managed to get a job with a Community Trust working with people with emotional and behavioural difficulties. It was challenging but brilliant.

The Trust owned a big house with eight bedrooms, providing sheltered accommodation for people who had recently left the local Mental Health Unit. I was one of a team of support workers, doing jobs like supervising meals and chaperoning people to their appointments with the doctor, the dentist or the Community Health Department. The residents included people suffering from schizophrenia and others with unpredictable behaviour – we had people who smashed windows, threw furniture around or lit fires. You had to be alert all the time.

One of my particular charges was Gwilym, a giant of a man (he was six foot seven) who had learning difficulties. One day I was taking a group for a walk to the local Day Centre when Gwilym ran off, waving his arms in the air and shouting. I tried to follow, forgetting that my amputated feet meant that I couldn't run properly. I was left behind and lost sight of him as he disappeared round a corner. Gwilym was never violent but he could be an alarming sight – we could hear people screaming as he passed. I finally caught up with him in the local park: he was sitting peacefully in the rose garden, playing with the soil.

One night I was helping him have a bath when I heard a commotion downstairs. Our new care assistant, Dave, looked like a pretty tough guy (I knew he worked as a bouncer at weekends), but now I could hear him yelling for help. When I got there I found that John, another resident, had thrown his dinner across the room. There was spaghetti bolognese all over the walls, and John was holding Dave by the throat. I grabbed John and threw him out of the back door into the garden, and started picking up the plates. When I turned round, I saw that

Gwilym had followed me downstairs, and was standing in the doorway stark naked! Dave left the next day – he couldn't stand the surreal pace of life.

A few nights later a new worker turned up – this time it was a young woman, really petite and fragile looking.

"Oh, no!" I thought. "When it all kicks off tonight, I'll be on my own. She won't be any help."

Sure enough, when I was putting another resident to bed I heard a racket downstairs, so I hurried to the rescue. To my surprise, I found her pinning John down in the correct restraint position – containing but not hurting him – and everything was under control. I realized then that it wasn't physical strength you needed, but knowledge and a calm and confident attitude. She was a great colleague.

I worked in that home for around eighteen months, and on the whole I was very happy there. Unfortunately I took a lot of stick from Gary, the manager, about my faith. He used to say to me, "Look at these guys. They're damaged goods. How can your God allow this? Where is your God now?" I felt oppressed by his cynicism.

We had one resident called Michael, who was in his fifties but had a mental age of about ten. One day he asked if he could come to church with me, so I said I'd get permission. I went to Gary and asked if it would be OK.

"Are you winding me up?" he answered. "What's the point?"

"Never mind – is it OK to take him? I'll pick him up and bring him back."

"OK, if you think it's worth it," he said.

Michael loved it – he joined in with the singing and clapping, and didn't exhibit any of his usual bizarre behaviour for the whole service. I thought of the words of Psalm 8:2: "From the lips of children and infants you have ordained praise."

The next day when we were all in the garden, Gary kept mimicking Michael's way of moving his hands, and teasing him by shouting "Hallelujah, Michael!" Then he leaned back in his chair, raised his arms and shouted to the sky, "God, you don't exist!"

A week later he got the sack for some irregularities of procedure while he was in charge. I felt sorry for him, but I couldn't help feeling that God was not prepared to be mocked, or have Michael's innocence ridiculed in that way. I happened to be standing in the hall as Gary left the building. I was surprised when he spoke to me as he passed.

"Pray for me, Peter," he said.

"I will," I replied.

Who knows where those prayers might lead?

So life went on. I was working hard. It wasn't the life I'd imagined when I left Bible College, but then, at one stage neither had I imagined that I would be planning marriage to a beautiful girl. I was truly blessed.

October came, and a few days before the wedding Sarah's friends and family started arriving from Switzerland. There was no large hotel in Sandbach, and there were so many visitors, we couldn't think where they could all stay. I mentioned the problem to Stuart, my landlord, and he came up with an unexpected solution. He put a bunch of keys on the table.

"Here's the keys to my house. I'll go away for a few days, and they can all move in. The only thing I ask is that you don't touch the vintage wines!"

I was astounded. Stuart lived in a massive seven-bedroom house, and there was room for everyone. As you can imagine, they looked after that house with loving care, and left it immaculate.

We had hardly any money, but it didn't seem to matter; we were surrounded by generosity. A lady in Switzerland gave Sarah her wedding dress as a gift – it was absolutely stunning. Sometimes, when God blesses you, he really pours it out.

Our wedding day dawned sunny and fine. Sarah was getting ready at a friend's house, helped by her mother and sisters. The church was filling up with our Bible College friends from all over the world. My friend Adrian (the missionary from France) had stayed at the flat with me, and helped me to decorate the railings outside the church with white ribbons; Andrew from Bible College was going to sing for us; George Laguda from Nigeria and my sister Annette would both read from the Bible; and Dr John Smith, the Principal, was going to lead the worship.

I sat nervously at the front of the church as the music started. I had longed for this moment for so long, and now it seemed to me that a series of miracles had finally brought us to this point. I looked round and saw Sarah entering the church: she looked like a princess, in her white dress and gloves and with a tiara sparkling in her golden hair.

I could hardly believe that this was happening to me. When the minister pronounced us man and wife I took my beautiful bride in my arms and kissed her, and our friend Andrew sang, "Love is made for two". We took hands and walked out of the church to the tune of "Amazing Grace" – the same song that had been playing that day when I walked down the aisle of another church to receive Jesus as my Saviour. Now I was walking towards the future together with my lovely wife. God had filled my cup until it was running over.

Chapter 9

Skilled and equipped

What I hadn't understood when I left college and when I took those first jobs in care homes, seemingly at random, was that nothing happens randomly in a life that has been surrendered to Christ. I took jobs because I was desperate for money, and because I thought I could do them. God sent me jobs because he knew what skills I still had to develop. I needed to gain more confidence in my own abilities; I needed to learn to understand people and their motivations; I needed to be able to communicate at every level, with people who were educated and articulate as well as with people whose understanding of the world was limited. Over the next few years, as well as giving me an income to support my family, my different jobs were to equip me with all those things.

Not long after our wedding I saw an advert in the *Church of England Newspaper*. The Coke Hole Trust, a drug and alcohol rehabilitation centre in Andover, wanted support workers. No qualifications were required, just compassion and a willingness to work hard. I reckoned my past experiences had given me both: I had always had to work harder than other people to overcome my problems, and I understood addiction from the inside. My time at Bible College had also improved my administrative and communication skills.

The only problem was that the centre was in Hampshire – unknown territory for both of us. So when I was invited for interview, Sarah came with me to look around. While we were there we drafted an advertisement for the local church bulletin, asking for accommodation. If I was lucky enough to get the job, we would need somewhere to live.

The phone call offering me the post came a day or two later, but the start date was in two weeks' time! We started praying in earnest, trusting that we could use the issue of finding somewhere to live in the same way that Gideon used the fleeces he spread out overnight: he asked God to send him a sign by keeping the fleeces dry when the earth around them was wet with dew. I had learned the hard way how foolish it was to try to make changes in my life without making sure, through constant prayer, that I was acting according to God's will. So we asked God to show us that he wanted me to take the job by providing us with accommodation.

One week later the phone rang. It was a lady called Jenny from Andover Baptist Church, offering us a two-bedroom flat just round the corner from the Coke Hole Trust. I explained that although I had been offered a job, the wages were low.

"That's all right," replied this wonderful Christian lady. "I'll fix the rent to what you can afford."

I accepted her offer on the spot, even though we hadn't seen the flat. We were so sure that this had come from God, we were jumping for joy!

We shared our move with another couple we knew, who were also moving south at the same time. It shows you how little we owned when I say that we shared a white van, and there was room for our things in the back quarter of the van. We set off down the M6 feeling like Abraham setting out for Canaan. When we were dropped off at our destination we wondered for a moment whether we'd got the right address: it was a beautiful old manor house which had been converted into five flats. We were going to be very comfortable indeed.

My job was to support people who were recovering from drug or alcohol dependency. That meant joining them in leisure activities, taking them to appointments, and organizing their daily lives. When people come off drugs they need help to manage their life and introduce new routines – for instance, getting up in the morning and eating breakfast instead of sleeping all day. I also had to take part in the group work designed to help them examine their motivation for staying clean. I was the key worker for three people at a time, and before they went home every weekend I used to help them work out a strategy to prevent their relapse once they were back among their old haunts, with the people who used to supply them.

I remember sitting down one Friday with a guy called Michael and asking him what his plans were. They sounded OK.

"First off I'm going to get to the station without going into an off-licence," he said. "Then I'm getting a friend who doesn't take drugs to meet me off the train and get me home, so I don't pick up any gear on the way."

I wished him well, but when I got into work on Monday I heard some stark news: Michael was dead. His parents had found him in his room with all the equipment for using heroin

– it must have been an extra-strong batch, or he had lost some of his resistance to the drug by staying off it for a few weeks. Either way, it had killed him. Poor Michael. He knew all the right words to say, and he believed he was sincere, but the deep motivation to get clean just wasn't there, and he succumbed to temptation. I was deeply upset by Michael's death. He was an intelligent, gifted young man who had been deceived by the high he got from alcohol and drugs – in the end his life was not only blighted but taken by substance misuse.

The group work at the Trust was based on the Twelve-Step Programme operated by Alcoholics Anonymous and Narcotics Anonymous. It's a good programme: it requires honesty on the part of the addicts, and encourages them to be open to a power beyond themselves. It's a great stepping stone, and can start people out on the road of seeking God. But I saw over and over again that the programme was what the addicts relied on. It was their support, and as soon as they left it behind, their resolve would crumble. I never saw anyone come out of addiction both clean and restored unless they had also given their life to Jesus in an honest and sincere way. He gave them the power to stay off whatever substances they were abusing. Others tried and failed, relapsing time and time again. Even though everyone in the home was supposed to be committed to recovery, every week someone would try to smuggle drink, cannabis or heroin back onto the premises. All their lives were constantly on this tipping point between recovery and relapse.

Life at the Coke Hole Trust was always challenging. People withdrawing from addiction are often edgy and aggressive, and frequently suffer from paranoia. I often had to break up fights between residents, or get between two people armed with knives. In addition I was working shifts, which is stressful in itself. After two years or so, I thought I was at risk of "burnout", so I started scanning the job adverts in the papers.

One of the first to leap out at me was a vacancy for an egg-picker on the nearby Leckford Estate, which supplied the Waitrose supermarkets. I knew nothing about farming or eggs, but I distinctly felt God saying to me, "I want you to apply for this one."

It seemed crazy to me – I was sure the first thing they would say was that I was overqualified – but obediently I applied and was invited for interview. The village was beautiful, set in idyllic English countryside, but I still didn't know what a city boy like me was doing there. I handed the whole thing over to God.

"You brought me here, Lord," I said. "Do what you want with this interview."

When I went into the office, the guy there picked up my CV and read it: Bible College, experience in residential homes. With his eyes still on the paper he said, "Why are you applying for this job?"

That was when I knew the answer.

"I'm not," I replied. "I'm a Christian, and I believe I've been sent here to tell you that God loves you."

There was a long pause, and when he looked up at me I saw that his eyes were full of tears. He told me that he had been a Christian, but he had abandoned his faith years ago. We had a long, deep talk together, and at the end he smiled and shook my hand warmly. There was no more discussion of the egg-picking job.

It took courage for me to step out in faith like that, with the clear risk of being laughed at and thought a fool. But for me it was confirmation that one day God would have a role for me as his messenger.

Meanwhile, Sarah had been working at Lloyds Bank in Andover until we discovered that she was pregnant. We were elated when we knew we were going to be parents, and fortunately she had an easy pregnancy. Our daughter Amy was born in Salisbury Hospital in July 1999. When she was first put in my arms I couldn't help praying and praising God for this precious gift. Sarah and I just sat and gazed at her – she was so tiny and so perfect. We were happy to be a family, and we both knew we wanted more children. Eighteen months later our wonderful son Joel was born, and in 2003 our lovely daughter Jessica.

My next job was at nearby Enham Alamein, so named because the estate was originally bought by a charity to house, rehabilitate and employ men injured in the First World War. It was now a residential centre for people with physical and learning difficulties, but on a much larger scale than anything I had seen before. It was a whole community, with around 100 houses and flats, workshops, shops and its own Post Office. I was a Supervisor for people working in factories, both on and off the site; I sometimes took people out for work experience in other places, so they could be introduced to the normal working environment as well as the sheltered one at Enham. Many of our residents would enrol for an NVQ while they were working – earning a certificate in "Work Skills" gave them purpose and encouragement. To support this I qualified as an NVQ assessor.

It was another good job, and it gave me a rest from the volatile atmosphere of the Coke Hole. It also paid enough for us to buy our first little house in Ludgershall, a pleasant village just over the border in Wiltshire. I realized that I was building on my skills in the care environment and gaining experience all the time.

However, I was never content with too quiet a life, and though Enham was a happy place to work for a couple of years, it didn't present me with the challenges I had grown used to. One day I overheard my boss talking about a job being advertised with the Probation Service. I bought the local paper and found it for myself: they were looking for Support Workers for their Community Service Programmes (now called Unpaid Work). They needed someone with a D32-D33 qualification to assess offenders who had enrolled for an NVQ in relation to Health and Safety at Work. This was exactly the qualification I had gained for my job at Enham. It had my name on it! I knew I could work with people from difficult backgrounds – I came from one myself – and I'd been helping people with social and behavioural difficulties for years.

The interview went well until I was asked the question I had been dreading: "Have you ever been convicted of a criminal offence?"

"Well, that's that," I thought. I took a deep breath and explained about my youthful criminal career. I was sure they wouldn't want me now.

"Oh, that's all right," said one of the interviewers airily.

"You've got no serious offending in your record — those are all petty crimes, and from a long time ago. You'll be able to relate all the better to some of our offenders."

It was the first time I'd seen my criminal past as an added qualification! The job was a two-year placement, not a permanent post: the Probation Service had received money from the European Social Fund to run this project to award NVQs. It meant there were detailed objectives and criteria for success to be met.

My job was to visit the sites where the offenders had been sent to work — usually schools, churches or parks where the managers had agreed to have supervised offenders working for them — and assess their progress. Many of the offenders had never achieved anything at school, and usually this NVQ certificate was their first ever qualification. I always made a great point of encouraging them at the end of their placement, telling them how valuable it was to employers to have staff with a Health and Safety at Work certificate, and shaking their hand and saying, "Well done."

I usually did three or four visits a day, then went back to complete the paperwork at the office. At the end of the two years the Probation Service managers were very pleased with the results. All the targets had been met, the processes had been audited and approved and all the certificates awarded. I got a congratulatory phone call from my manager.

"And by the way," he added, "we'd like to offer you a permanent job with the Probation Service."

"Whereabouts?" I asked.

"Winchester Prison."

I didn't hesitate. "I'll take it," I said.

I sat in my office and thanked God. In 1995, when I left Bible College, I had tried to push my way into prison work, with no response. The timing was wrong. Sometimes God doesn't say "No" in answer to our prayers, but "Wait." Now the timing was right, and I had more experience and better skills in dealing with people than I had possessed nine years previously.

When I walked up to the prison gates that day I was thinking, "I am here by the grace of God." I didn't have to worry about what I would find behind those walls, because I had already been there – but this time I was free to leave when I wanted. What a privilege it was to be able to see both sides. How was it possible for someone with my background and my history of offending, who had been in prison, who had been homeless and slept on park benches, to be working here as a Probation Service Officer?

The job involved sentence management. When a prisoner had been sentenced to more than four years, I had to organize appropriate activities, ensure that he had access to the right programmes, and when he was moved on from the remand centre at Winchester, to ensure that his programme moved with him. The days are long gone when prisoners sat in their cells for twenty hours a day. Now there are all sorts of activities to meet their educational and social needs, designed to prepare them to cope better in the outside world when they are finally released.

Winchester offered courses in literacy and numeracy, computer skills, physical fitness, drug and alcohol rehabilitation and sex offender programmes. I had to identify the needs of the offenders, usually by taking them through the Pre-Sentence

Report prepared by the Probation Service, which describes the background to their offending behaviour, and their educational and employment history. Then we would discuss possible programmes to help them. I had to be encouraging and positive, because none of these activities could be imposed on the prisoners – they had to choose to do them.

I was also involved in the Home Detention Curfew system, when prisoners were released on licence to serve the remainder of their sentence under supervision in the community, with an electronic tag to monitor their whereabouts. On those occasions I would sit with the Prison Governor discussing individual prisoners and their suitability for release. I was the one who knew whether they were clean or had managed to get access to drugs in prison, and whether or not they had shown commitment to their sentence plan. I felt a bit like Joseph in the Bible, when he was moved from the prison cell to the palace, becoming adviser to the king.

God had opened the door for me to work in the prison, and I was thankful that I had fulfilled that dream. After a couple of years of working successfully with prisoners, I began to aspire to another role. I wanted to see where all these sentences started – in the court. This time I saw my next job advertised in an internal bulletin circulated within the Probation Service: it was for a Probation Service Officer in the Crown Court. Again I prayed first, offering God my willingness to learn new skills, but also my obedience if this wasn't within his will. I got the job.

This time I had even more responsibility, running the Probation activities in the court, and doing everything except writing the Pre-Sentence Reports themselves. I noticed the difference in the level of professionalism required at once. In the prison, I used to turn up for work wearing casual trousers, a shirt and jumper. Now I was expected to look smart in a suit and tie, showing respect for the dignity and importance of the court proceedings.

If a defendant pleaded not guilty to a charge, a trial date would be set. If he pleaded guilty, the court would often require four weeks for a Pre-Sentence Report to be compiled, giving the background to the case and the defendant's personal circumstances, and discovering whether he was suitable for certain sentencing options. My job was to provide the court with as much information as possible about the offender, including preparing "stand-down" reports (on the same day), assessing whether he was suitable for such disposals as drug or alcohol rehabilitation or unpaid work.

It was a demanding job. Adjournments were generally short, and I was kept running between court, office and interview rooms, talking to offenders or grabbing the relevant files and standing up in court to tell the judge how the individual had responded to previous sentences.

On one occasion the court was packed, and the judge and the Crown Prosecutor were engaged in a complex discussion, so I was relaxing at my desk at the back. Suddenly the judge asked me about the legal position on a certain disposal, and when I admitted that I didn't know the answer, he told me to go away and look it up. I found myself in the Probation Office consulting a huge tome full of technical legal detail in minute print, and I had another one of those "How did I get here?" moments. If my school teachers – who had generally given up on getting me to read anything more demanding than the *Beano* – could see me now! Judges often called me to their chambers when they were deliberating about a disposal, to ask my opinion. I think they liked my down-to-earth, pragmatic approach, and the fact that I managed to get to know the offenders fairly thoroughly. They nearly always accepted my advice.

One day in court I learned a powerful lesson. The judge was pronouncing sentence and he said, "I really don't want to send you to prison. It pains me. I would love to give you another chance. But the law compels me to send you into custody for this offence."

I suddenly realized that God is like this. He is a God of love, of mercy and of grace, but he will carry out a judgment one day. He takes no pleasure in seeing a sinner perish, and longs for him to change. But sometimes, if that sinner rejects every offer of mercy, there is no option. The outcome is inevitable, and the man has chosen for himself.

My life outside work was busy, too. One evening I was leaving home to drive to church in Andover, when I noticed the usual group of teenagers hanging around on the street. There was nothing in the village for them to do, and they couldn't afford the fare to go into the nearby towns.

"Why am I driving off to a church meeting somewhere else?" I thought. "There's a real need here."

I knew plenty of people from Andover Baptist Church who lived in or around the village. We got together to discuss the problem, and the result was a new youth club called Teen Reach.

We put together a plan and managed to secure a Lottery grant of £12,000. With that we bought music equipment, computers and games, and hired the village Scout Hall which had a good kitchen. In no time we had sixty to seventy kids attending our Thursday evening meetings, playing table tennis, snooker, pool or basketball, and running discos or just hanging out with their friends. We got people in to give talks – police, probation and prison officers – and we took the kids out for trips, including motorcycle training. They loved it, and it provided a Christian witness in the village.

Meanwhile there were other changes in our lives. In 2006, when all three children were at school or pre-school, Sarah found that she once again had some time on her hands. I was working happily at the Crown Court, and it was time for her to fulfil one of her dreams. She had always wanted to run a coffee shop or tea shop – she is a wonderful cook, and the Swiss pastries she produces are amazing: light, crumbly and delicious. The Christians in our village needed a meeting-place, and they wanted somewhere which would act as a lighthouse for Christ. We saw how these things could be combined. We found suitable premises, and got a business loan to pay for the cost of the equipment for a professional kitchen. Local Christians helped us to fit it out, and Café Oasis was in business. It is open from 8.30 in the morning (for the breakfast and coffee-on-the-way-to-work trade) to 4.30 in the afternoon (when Sarah goes home to care for the children), with bistro-style lunches served in the middle of the day. It quickly gained a reputation among the local people, and always seemed to be buzzing with activity.

One night after Teen Reach, a fourteen-year-old lad called

Billy came up to me. He looked a bit down, and I asked him if he was OK. By then we had built up a bit of a rapport, and I knew he trusted me.

"Can I be honest?" he asked. "I'm hooked on drugs. I'm drinking too much. I have sex with my girlfriend but it's a let-down. I'm always high on something. I'm really depressed."

My heart felt crushed. All that – and he was only fourteen! I remembered my own childhood so vividly, and I knew his background. It wasn't too different from mine. He lived on a scruffy council estate where there was high unemployment, high crime rates, a high incidence of absent fathers and no boundaries for the kids, a lot of teenage sex, and too many drug dealers. I looked at his sad young face, and thought, "Unless someone intervenes in this lad's life, he'll end up in prison, in drug rehab, or dead." All the stepping-stones were there, and he was on the road to disaster.

"I've got no answers for you, Billy, except one," I said. "I'm a Christian, and I know Jesus was the only one who could get me out of a situation like yours. Can I pray for you?"

"Yes, please," he said.

I didn't push him too hard. I didn't preach at him. I just asked God to protect and guide him, and bring him safely through all the dangers he was living in. I knew Billy was moving away in a couple of weeks, and I didn't know if I would ever see him again, but I often thought about him and prayed for him, wherever he might be.

Four years later a guy in army gear walked into the Bistro while I was serving. He was so tall he had to stoop to get through the door – he must have been six foot six at least. It took me a few minutes before I recognized him.

He came up to the counter and called to me, "Peter!"

"Billy!" I exclaimed. "It's great to see you!"

We sat down with a cup of coffee and he told me his story.

"I'll never forget that day you prayed for me. Thank God, things picked up for me after that. Moving house took me away from the drug dealers, and as soon as I was old enough I joined the army. I got off the drugs and the drink, and trained up to get fit enough to pass the entry requirements. I've travelled the world, I've got good mates, and I like the discipline."

He looked great – fit, healthy and happy. I thanked God that my prayers had been answered and Billy had gone the right way. God had laid out a path for him to walk on safely into adulthood.

It was fantastic to see prayers answered like that, and I could see that working in the café opened the way to conversations in the same way as the youth club did. I had seen so many of my prayers answered and my dreams fulfilled, and I began wondering what else God might have in store for me. I had always known that there was a calling on my life, and I had always suspected that God would one day want me to work in full-time ministry – I just hadn't expected it to take so long to come about. But I had learned my lesson now, and I was willing to wait on God's timing, not my own impatience.

What I hadn't expected was the time of testing that awaited us as a family.

Chapter 10

Into the future

One day I was sitting in my office at the Crown Court when I distinctly felt that God was saying to me, "Don't get too comfortable here. This is only temporary." Sure enough, within a few weeks there were a couple of incidents which made me begin to question whether I wanted to carry on in the same job. They were no more than the minor irritations of any job, really – for instance, the complex processes which required me to drive forty miles just because someone had forgotten to sign a document. There were no major problems, but events began to confirm in my mind that it was time to move on. Six months later I gave in my notice and joined Sarah in running Café Oasis.

My decision was helped by the fact that we needed more help in the café: the business had grown in the three years since its opening. It's situated on the busy main road in Ludgershall High Street, so there's plenty of passing trade for morning coffee, afternoon tea, and also for the lunchtime sandwiches, soups, salads and desserts on offer. All the food is made freshly on the day, and the cooker is behind the bar so people can see their meal being prepared.

Our aim for the café was always that it should be a place of refreshment in every sense, where people could meet and talk as well as eat and drink. There are four shops in the same unit, and the other shopkeepers know that we're Christians, so we have every opportunity to be a light in our local community. Local Christians meet for fellowship over tea and coffee, and friendships grow and are strengthened.

It's also a medium for ministry. I believe that I have a specific ministry not only to preach and teach, but also to use the prophetic gifts which have been recognized by the church. This doesn't happen every day, but often I find that I have been used in ways which I can't explain except as the purpose of God.

One night I had a strange dream about a house in Andover which had been flooded. I could clearly see the water in the back garden, though the front of the house looked OK. When I woke up I couldn't get the dream out of my head – it persisted, no matter how hard I tried to put it aside. When I went to open up the café I told Sarah about it, and she suggested I ask God for the interpretation. At about eleven o'clock a man came in and ordered a sandwich. The café was quiet, so I chatted to him as I was making it.

"Are you just passing through?" I asked.

"Oh, yes, I'm on my way to Andover, to do a job there. I'm a flood assessor."

My hands stopped still over the bread and butter – I was arrested by the Holy Spirit.

"Why, what's happened?" I said.

"There's a house there whose garden's been flooded."

I knew then that the dream had been warning me of this man's arrival, and was the sign I needed that this was the person God wanted me to speak to. Even so, you can't just bombard people with your faith – you have to be sensitive and respectful, or they won't be willing to listen to you at all. 1 Peter 3:15 says: "Always be prepared to give an answer to everyone who asks you to give the reason for the hope that you have." I had to find the right words to explain my faith and the message I felt I had for this man.

I finished making his sandwich and said, "Can I be honest with you? I had this dream last night…"

The man got up from his table and came over to the bar to listen, and I shared the message of hope and renewal that Jesus offers us. Moments later the man was in tears and asking Jesus into his life. When he finally paid for his sandwich and took it away, he stood in the doorway and said, "Thank you for talking to me."

"God bless you," I told him.

A year later he called in again, specially to tell me that he had joined a church and was going forward with God in his life. It was yet another confirmation that God uses me in a prophetic way to reach people, and that I am walking in a pathway prepared by God.

This reassurance became even more important to us both just after Christmas 2009. We were travelling to Switzerland to spend a holiday with Sarah's family, and we had a terrible journey. Eurostar trains had broken down in the Channel Tunnel, and we had to wait at Ashford station for eight hours. The children were exhausted and Sarah looked shattered before we even got to France. The weather was very bad and we drove to her home in Brienz, a little lakeside town, in blizzard conditions.

When we finally got to bed Sarah looked pale and ill, but I assumed it was just tiredness. Then she turned to me and said, "Peter, I can feel a lump in my stomach."

My heart lurched. We knew she couldn't be pregnant. The next day she went to the family doctor, who did a blood test. When he called us back into his surgery he spoke English for my benefit.

"I have bad news for you. The lumps are almost certainly tumours. You must go straight to the hospital where they will do some more tests, and come back here at 6.30 this evening for the results."

We were numb with shock, but over and over again in those days I was thankful that we were in Switzerland when Sarah became ill. In England we could have waited for weeks for a diagnosis, time in which her condition would have deteriorated further.

We hurried to the hospital in nearby Interlaken where Sarah underwent more tests and saw a radiologist. Then we came home and waited for our evening appointment. It was a bad few hours. Outside the doctor's surgery that evening we stood in the rain and wept together before God, praying for the strength and courage to face whatever the future held.

The doctor told us that it was definitely cancer: Sarah would have to go to the specialist hospital in Berne for another scan. Depending on the results, she could then decide whether to return to the UK or stay in Switzerland.

The first news from the second scan was not encouraging – the doctors couldn't confirm where the tumour originated, so they recommended a biopsy. If the results showed that the tumour was benign, they would remove it. The end of our holiday was coming up, so we decided that I would go home to reopen the café. I was worried but also relieved that at least Sarah was getting the best possible care. Three days later I had a phone call saying that the operation was successful and that the doctors had removed two large tumours from Sarah's abdomen as well as one ovary. The test results showed that the cancer was benign. We were overjoyed and relieved that the ordeal was finally over.

A week later Sarah had an appointment with the doctor to remove the stitches and to get a travel certificate to say that she was fit to fly home. She was shocked to be told that further detailed tests on the tumours indicated Non-Hodgkin's Lymphoma, a highly aggressive and malignant form of cancer. I closed the café and flew straight back to Brienz.

Sarah recovered well from the operation and we all flew home together a few weeks later. The children thought the doctors had made Mummy better, but we knew that she still had to face the trial of undergoing six courses of chemotherapy. That was hard: she suffered all the usual side-effects, including losing all her beautiful hair. She faced this with typical cheerfulness, getting me to shave her head from the outset. If she was going to lose her hair, she was going to be the one in control!

Throughout the treatment she always stayed positive, trusting in God to see her through every difficulty. Not long ago one of our regular customers, who isn't a Christian, called in at the café with a gift for Sarah.

"You guys are a blessing to have in this village," she said.

"You've gone through so much pain and illness this year, and you've always kept going, and you always seem to be smiling."

Sarah herself puts this resilience down to God. After the first couple of chemo treatments, she knew what to expect, and she would come home from hospital knowing the fatigue and nausea that awaited her. When she felt physically ill and emotionally drained she would cry out to God, and he always answered her prayers, filling her with that deep joy and security that comes from knowing we are safe in the Father's hands. The bad week she was expecting simply failed to materialize. Instead, the Holy Spirit gave her courage, strength and joy.

We were nervous when we went for her first review appointment. We sat in the waiting-room with the children, praying that the tests would show that the cancer had gone. The doctor called us in and said, "You can bring the children with you." I knew then that it was going to be good news.

"All the tests indicate that your cancer is in remission," she said. "No further treatment is necessary."

It was a massive release of all the tension, and we hugged each other in joy. It was like coming up out of a year-long dark tunnel, into the sunlight.

The children were thrilled, too. We had been honest with them from the outset, explaining after the first doctor's appointment that Mummy wasn't well and had got something called cancer. Jessica cried; Joel, who is usually very bubbly and active, went very quiet. Amy, the oldest, was the only one who understood much about what it might mean, and she asked the crucial question: "Is Mummy going to die?"

"We don't know what's going to happen," I told her,

"but we're all going to pray together. Just because bad things happen, it doesn't mean that God has taken his hands off us. We're trusting him to look after Mummy and all of us."

We continued with that attitude throughout Sarah's treatment, praying with the children and asking for God's protection. Because they have grown up in faith, they are used to taking all their troubles to Jesus. Joel, in particular, seems to have a developing relationship with God. One day after we had been reading about the disciples' experience at Pentecost, we prayed together as a family for the Holy Spirit to fill us. Joel started crying. I knew something was going on in him, but I didn't bother him with questions. Later that evening, I asked him if he wanted to tell me about it.

"It was like I was standing by a waterfall, Daddy, and I looked up and saw a beautiful white house in heaven. Then I looked down and I could see all the people in hell."

"Keep looking up, son," I said. "Keep looking to God."

The children all know the story of my life, and how I came to find Jesus. When I first wrote down my own account of what happened to me, Amy couldn't bear to read it – she said it made her too sad. I explained that when you trust God, he brings you through all the pain and suffering into his beautiful joy. I believe it's very important that we build the foundations of our family life on our faith in Christ, so that the children grow up knowing Jesus and trusting him.

As we look to the future, we continue to trust God for Sarah's health, and for our growing family. We are waiting to see where God will take us next. Our church has been encouraging me to explore the possibilities for full-time work in Christian ministry, and we have felt for some time that this is where God is leading me. He has invested a lot in our lives, and we want to be used as he chooses. We don't know what the next chapter will be; I only know what God has promised me: "'For I know the plans I have for you,' declares the Lord, 'plans to prosper you and not to harm you, plans to give you hope and a future'" (Jeremiah 29:11).

I have always felt that my primary calling is to evangelism, and as I look back to the various jobs I have done, I realize how carefully God was leading me to develop my gifts and to learn new skills, so that when I am talking to people I can get alongside them and understand other points of view. I believe that every encounter with another human being is precious, whether they are hurt and damaged physically, mentally or emotionally, whether they are addicted to drink or drugs or crime, or whether they are outwardly successful and competent but inwardly lost. There is always something that God can touch and make new.

What does seem to be developing at the moment is a speaking ministry, and I am often asked to visit churches to give my testimony and teach on the subject of prophetic evangelism, when God asks you to pass on divine revelation to another person. Sometimes he speaks directly to individuals, and sometimes to an intermediary who can pass the message on, but it always seems to have a tremendously encouraging effect – not only on the person receiving the message, but also on the messenger and on the rest of the faithful congregation where this ministry is in use.

A good biblical example of this is Peter's vision on the rooftop:

He became hungry and wanted something to eat, and while the meal was being prepared, he fell into a trance. He saw heaven opened and something like a large sheet being let down to earth by its four corners. It contained all kinds of four-footed animals, as well as reptiles of the earth and birds of the air. Then a voice told him, "Get up, Peter. Kill and eat."

"Surely not, Lord," Peter replied. "I have never eaten anything impure or unclean."

The voice spoke to him a second time, "Do not call anything impure that God has made clean."

Acts 10:10–15

So when Peter was called to go to the house of a Gentile named Cornelius, he didn't refuse, as he could have done, on the grounds that "it is against our law for a Jew to associate with a Gentile or visit him." Instead, he said, "But God has shown me that I should not call any man impure or unclean" (Acts 10:28). This opened the way for Peter to preach the gospel, not only to Cornelius, but also to the large crowd of Gentile friends he had gathered. And as the final sign, God caused the Holy Spirit to fall on the Gentile converts, a blessing which astonished the Jewish believers who had accompanied Peter. They all received the important message that God's kingdom was for everyone, not just the Jews.

I want to encourage the church to understand that

prophetic evangelism is a gift of God. We read about this in Ephesians 4:11–12:

> *It was he who gave some to be apostles, some to be prophets, some to be evangelists, and some to be pastors and teachers, to prepare God's people for works of service, so that the body of Christ may be built up…*

Prophetic evangelism is part of the office of the prophet. If you receive this gift you should not expect to be used in this fashion every day, or for everyone you meet. But it is an important gift, and I believe all Christians have the potential to exercise it.

A recent development is the contact I have made with a beautiful and amazing lady called Katie Piper. Her life was changed for ever when acid was thrown in her face, and she suffered terrible burns. As she recovered, she suffered trauma and deep insecurity because of the change in her physical appearance, but there seemed to be very little support available. In response, she set up the Katie Piper Foundation to make a difference to burns victims, developing new treatments and therapies, providing psychological and social support networks, and working towards greater acceptance within society.

When I heard about her plans, I was immediately reminded of my encounter with Paul, the young man who was burned in a car accident. I contacted him again some months later, and found him transformed. He still bore those terrible scars, but he had a new faith, a new job and a new girlfriend – and he smiled. I knew that meeting someone who understood his situation had made a huge difference to him. Once again I can see how God has prepared me for the work he wants me to do, and how he can use even the worst experience to bring about something good. (If you would like to find out more about Katie's work, go to www.katiepiperfoundation.org.uk.)

I am always happy to speak about what God has done in my life. The story told in this book has a message of hope for all the people who have lived chaotic lives, the marginalized and those in despair, who believe that their lives are worthless and meaningless. It shows that there is a way out of the darkness into light, through having a relationship with God, who tells us that he has come that we may have life, and have it abundantly. When I share what God has done for me, I want to show that he can do it for you, too.

I have tried to be honest in this book; I have opened my heart and made myself vulnerable. It's easy enough for Christians to say, "I did these bad things before I became a Christian, but I'm different now." It's much harder to say, "I gave my life to Christ but I still made mistakes and let him down, because sometimes the old habits were just too strong for me." But this is the reality, and I felt that I had to be transparent about the spiritual battles that continue even after you have become a Christian. Too often people are put off by a "holier than thou" attitude on the part of the church, as though everyone inside it is perfect, looking down patronizingly on the poor sinners outside. The truth is that we're all in it together, and often Christians behave just as badly as everyone else. "If we claim to be without sin, we deceive ourselves and the truth is not in us" (1 John 1:8). But we know the inspiring verse which follows: "If we confess our sins, he is faithful and just and will forgive us our sins and purify us from all unrighteousness" (1 John 1:9). The Christian life is a constant striving to stay in God's will. Of course we fail sometimes, but by the power of the Holy Spirit we are able to pick ourselves up, learn our lesson, and try again, because the rewards are infinite.

Psalm 107 has always been close to my heart, because it sounds as if it was written by someone who understands my story:

> *Some sat in darkness and the deepest gloom,*
> *prisoners suffering in iron chains,*
> *for they had rebelled against the words of God*
> *and despised the counsel of the Most High…*
> *Then they cried to the Lord in their trouble,*
> *and he saved them from their distress…*
>
> *Some became fools through their rebellious ways*
> *and suffered affliction because of their iniquities…*
> *Then they cried to the Lord in their trouble,*
> *and he saved them from their distress.*

Psalm 107:10–19

The repeated refrain in this psalm, "and he saved them from their distress", exactly describes what God did for me. "He brought them out of darkness and the deepest gloom and broke away their chains" (Psalm 107:14), just as he did mine. Thank you, Lord.

When I became a Christian that day in 1989, I understood

very little of what the Christian life was about. I only knew that I had been offered a lifeline of hope, and I grabbed it. You don't need to know any theology to become a Christian, you just need a heart that's open to God, and a willingness to surrender your life to him. It's a private deal between you and God: you don't need to fill in an application form or write your CV, because he already knows the secrets of your heart. If you would like to take that first step into new life, you might like to say this simple prayer:

Jesus, I understand that God wants me to know his love, and joy, and peace.
But I feel a long way from God, because I know I don't live the way he wants. I've messed things up in my life. Please forgive me.
Thank you for coming and showing us God's love. I want you to guide my life and show me your power. Please fill me with your Holy Spirit and show me the way to follow you. Amen.

God preserved me when I was a tiny baby, lying helpless on a burning hearth-rug in a Halifax council house. He watched over me when I was a lost young man, physically and emotionally scarred by my chaotic life. And he met me when I was at my lowest point and offered me a new way of living. He literally saved my life. He rescued me twice: the first time through the hands of that fireman who lifted me from the ashes of that house fire, and the second time through the words of my sister who spoke the promises of Jesus and brought me out of the ashes of shame, remorse and despair.

He can do the same for you. No matter what fires have burned in your life, no matter how much has been damaged or consumed by the flames, he can bring new life out of the ashes, and give you healing, hope and purpose.

* * *

If you would like to contact me about becoming a Christian or about anything you have read in this book, please email me at: peter@outofashes.co.uk

Jesus encourages us to minister in various ways to all kinds of lost and broken people. In particular, Matthew 25:36 says, "I was in prison and you visited me." We are currently working with chaplains and volunteers from Prison Fellowship England and Wales who request free copies to take into Britain's prisons. Would you consider sponsoring a copy of *Out of the Ashes* so that it can be given to a prisoner serving a prison sentence in the UK? If you can partner with us in this way, please contact us through our website www.outofashes.co.uk

Peter is also available for inspirational public speaking events. To book, email us at: speakingevent@outofashes.co.uk